DAILY LIFE IN

THE NEW
TESTAMENT

DAILY LIFE IN

THE NEW TESTAMENT

JAMES W. ERMATINGER

The Greenwood Press "Daily Life Through History" Series

GREENWOOD PRESS
Westport, Connecticut • London

Library of Congress Cataloging-in-Publication Data

Ermatinger, James William, 1959–
    Daily life in the New Testament / James W. Ermatinger.
        p. cm. — (Greenwood Press "Daily life through history"
    series, ISSN 1080–4749)
    Includes bibliographical references and index.
    ISBN 978–0–313–34175–5 (alk. paper)
    1. Church history—Primitive and early church, ca. 30–600.   2. Palestine—
Social life and customs—To 70 A.D.   3. Palestine—Civilization.   4. Rome—
History—Empire, 30 B.C.–476 A.D.   5. Jews—Social life and customs—
To 70 A.D.   I. Title.
    BR165.E76   2008
    225.9'5—dc22   2008001137

British Library Cataloguing in Publication Data is available.

Library of Congress Catalog Card Number: 2008001137
ISBN: 978–0–313–34175–5
ISSN: 1080–4749

First published in 2008

Greenwood Press, 88 Post Road West, Westport, CT 06881
An imprint of Greenwood Publishing Group, Inc.
www.greenwood.com

Printed in the United States of America

The paper used in this book complies with the
Permanent Paper Standard issued by the National
Information Standards Organization (Z39.48–1984).

10 9 8 7 6 5 4 3 2 1

To Michelle and Ian

CONTENTS

Acknowledgments ix

Introduction xi

Chronology xxv

1. Geographical and Historical Overview 1

2. Daily Life of Geographical Groups in Palestine 19

3. Nonreligious Influences: Language, Art, and Hellenistic Culture 31

4. Pre-Messianic Judaism: Worship and Temple Practices 43

5. Expectations of the Messiah 57

6. Trades and Professions 75

7. Rural Life and Urban Life 87

8. Family Life and Living Conditions 103

9. Roman Occupation 117

10. Conclusion 127

Glossary 137

Bibliography 139

Index 145

ACKNOWLEDGMENTS

I would like to thank Mariah Gumpert of Greenwood Press who suggested the work and encouraged me when I lagged behind, especially when I began my new job. I would like to acknowledge and thank Chris McGowen, dean of the College of Math and Science and interim dean of the College of Liberal Arts at Southeast Missouri State University, who provided financial help for traveling to libraries and museums. My daughter Michelle and son Ian continued to help me by asking questions and debating with me issues concerning religion and life. I would like to thank Mona Hughey who gave me encouragement and support. Although all of these individuals helped, I assume full responsibility for the material in this book. All attempts have been made to find the rightful copyright holders and if I have omitted or made a mistake please contact me so that I may rectify the error.

INTRODUCTION

The first century C.E. witnessed the development of a new religion, Christianity, and the political destruction of the Jewish state. These political and religious phenomena impacted society tremendously. At the same time society influenced the religious backdrop and the political evolution. This work attempts to examine these influences amid the political, social, economic, and religious background.

The daily life of individuals living during the first century C.E. in Palestine, Asia Minor, and the Eastern Mediterranean regions is a contrast of religions, ethnic groups, political powers, and social classes. The difference between the first century B.C.E. and the first century C.E. was tremendous. Politically Rome now controlled the region, a strong middle class enhanced the economic picture, and the spread, albeit small, of a new religion, Christianity, shaped daily life in 100 C.E.

The new religion began from Judaism but ultimately split to develop along different lines. Christianity was founded by the followers of Jesus, a Jew, who lived his life according to the Jewish customs and norms. The figure of Jesus is the most important character, because his life and teachings provided the initial force of the new religion. Jesus, however, is an enigma. The works that survive do not give a very complete picture of his life. While we may desire a biography, what is probably more important for modern readers of these surviving works is how Jesus was viewed by others.

By understanding how different groups viewed Jesus we are able to understand these groups, which shaped the daily lives of those coming into contact with believers of the new religion. An examination of the different groups—Jesus' followers, Jewish religious groups, Jewish political powers, Roman leaders, social elites, the middle class, and the common people—and how they viewed Jesus helps the modern reader understand daily life of the time of the New Testament.

JESUS' FOLLOWERS

In the New Testament different groups of Jesus' followers are mentioned. First there were the original 12 apostles or disciples. Even here there were clearly different ranks, which influenced the future religion. Clearly Simon Peter or Peter, along with James and John the sons of Zebedee, were Jesus' closest confidantes, at least according to the Gospels. In numerous passages these three figures, either individually or together, were constantly discussing, asking, and being asked questions by Jesus. After this small group the other apostles, usually just referred to as the "followers," had interactions with Jesus and others. After Jesus' death his followers went through a period of time in which they attempted to carry out Jesus' original mission of bringing his message to their fellow Jews. These followers clearly believed that Jesus was the Messiah (the anointed one), although what kind: political, military, religious, or social, was not clear. The original 12, less Judas Iscariot but increased with Matthias, began to preach his message in Palestine. Their belief was their strength.

These followers, however, also had different views of Jesus. For example, one disciple is referred to as Simon the Zealot, a reference to the political group that believed in the military victory over the Romans. Did this mean that he and others believed in armed conflict? It is impossible to know for sure, but some of Jesus' apostles, including Simon Peter, were armed and even used their weapons. After Jesus' death some of his disciples, notably James (either the son of Zebedee or the less) who became the recognized leader of the group in Jerusalem, established a structure in the religion. John the son of Zebedee established churches in the western region of Asia Minor. The followers, at least some, were capable of organizing themselves, showing some talent for creating an organization. The immediate followers then viewed Jesus as the Messiah, and after the violent persecutions of Herod Agrippa during the 40s C.E. they established a distinct religion.

In addition to this small intimate group, there were other followers who likewise traveled with Jesus and after his death remained with the 12. One of the most important groups was the women. Women were mentioned in several instances. The most important members included Jesus' mother Mary, Martha and her sister Mary, and Mary Magdalene. Mary Magdalene has traditionally been viewed as a sinner, a prostitute, but this portrait has recently been challenged. The more recent view is that she was in fact an important follower who helped Jesus financially. It has been argued that she was viewed as a sinner because some of the early Church leaders wanted to minimize her importance. Whether the traditional view is true or not, Mary was an important follower. The women were reportedly the first group that went to the tomb and proclaimed that Jesus had indeed risen from the dead. Other followers included individuals like Stephen, who was the first martyr, and Paul, originally named Saul, a former persecutor of the new religion. These individuals likewise viewed Jesus as the anointed one.

JEWISH RELIGIOUS GROUPS

The Jewish religious groups viewed Jesus in different ways. The major groups consisted of the Pharisees, Sadducees, and Essenes. The Pharisees had become the dominant religious group in Judea during the time of Jesus. Appealing to the masses, they were in fact representative of the majority of Jews. They had established and preached in the synagogues, believing that the Temple was not the only place for Judaism. Jesus, in fact, was probably educated by the Pharisees because they were the predominant group in Galilee, and many of his ideas were in fact Pharisaic. What bothered the Pharisees about Jesus was his claim to being God's son and his tolerance of his disciples' violating the Jewish dietary laws. For the Pharisees, Jesus' claim to divinity became the dominant point of antagonism against him. This antagonism can be seen in their continual ridicule of his origin from Galilee. The more common complaint was that Jesus' followers disobeyed the dietary rules, collecting grain on the Sabbath. Worse yet, Jesus did not agree with the Pharisees in their condemnation of his disciples. The Pharisees were in turn ridiculed by Jesus when he said that they were more concerned with their positions, rich robes, and glory than with the people.

The Pharisees believed in not upsetting the balance of power between the Jews and Rome. They would hate the Romans but tolerate them until the Messiah came. For the Pharisees Jesus could not be the Messiah because he was from Galilee. But Jesus and his followers did have similarities with the Pharisees that are important. For example, both Jesus and his followers argued for the resurrection of the body. The Pharisees had developed the idea that the body would rise; this view was taken by Jesus, and more importantly his followers, and became the central tenet of Christianity. With Jesus becoming more popular, the Pharisees viewed him as a potential threat to their hold on the people.

The Sadducees were rivals of the Pharisees, believing in the predominance of the Temple. As the central place of worship, the Temple symbolized Judaism. Unlike the Pharisees, the Sadducees did not believe in the resurrection of the body. Both the Sadducees' position with the Temple and the power of the high priest were dependent upon the Romans, who controlled Jerusalem and could appoint the high priest. In addition, the

Sadducees were the most conservative of the major religious groups. Although not as numerous as the Pharisees, the Sadducees nevertheless held the most power.

Jesus consistently argued against the Sadducees' position. Like the Pharisees, they attacked Jesus for keeping company with sinners and prostitutes; however, because they did not believe in the resurrection of the body they also attacked Jesus for his views on that subject. The Sadducees also ridiculed Jesus when he said that he would restore the Temple in three days (Mark 13:1–3). Although probably a later addition to the New Testament, the passage in which this argument appears nevertheless showed the contrasting views of the Sadducees and Jesus' followers. The Sadducees viewed Jesus with concern, because he advocated a different religious order, one against the power of the Temple.

A third group, the Essenes, probably did not have much contact with Jesus. As separatists who generally lived apart from society, they viewed Jewish religious society, namely the Sadducees, as traitors. Josephus (an early Jewish historian) related that they lived in many cities throughout Palestine but were mainly isolationists. Evidence suggests that they resided near the Dead Sea at Qumran. The archaeological and literary evidence reinforces the view that they were isolationists and misogynists. The Essenes practiced ritual cleansing, an idea preached by John the Baptist that Jesus later transformed into a cleansing of the soul. Although it is difficult to know how the Essenes viewed or would have viewed Jesus, most likely they would have viewed him with suspicion.

JEWISH POLITICAL POWERS

Within Judaism there were numerous groups that had different political agendas. Some believed in the violent overthrow of the Roman occupation force. One such group was the Zealot party. Although having some religious influences, the Zealots believed in a restored, independent Judean state. Traditionally, the Zealots were not seen as a fully formed group until after Jesus' birth. This view, however, may not be completely satisfactory. Some scholars argue that the Zealots may in fact have originated earlier during the reign of Herod the Great. This view is supported by Josephus, who viewed the Zealots as a nationalistic-religious force originating before the insurrection at the time of the Roman occupation in 6 C.E. The Zealots did not believe that Herod and his successors were legitimate Jewish rulers; their view often led to attacks against both Roman and Jewish troops and officials. Their nationalism was further strengthened by their religious devotion. Associated with the Zealots were the Sicarii or dagger men. Using stealth, they would strike in secrecy and attack their enemies. They were led by descendents of Judas of Galilee, who had led a revolt against Rome when Quirinius, the governor of Syria, arrived in Judea in 6 C.E. to carry out the census required for the new Roman province.

From a realistic point of view, the Zealots could not succeed by terror alone. Unlike modern states, Rome did not have to worry about bad public press, television, or the Internet. Roman policy was often to use brute force against civilians to turn them against their own rebels. In addition the political agenda was unrealistic because it required Rome to give up Palestine. One of Jesus' followers is reported to have been a Zealot, although this is not certain because the Greek could also be translated as "excited one." If, however, Simon the Zealot was part of the political group, it may also be that Judas Iscariot referred to him as not being from a region, but rather as a follower of the Sicarii.[1] Whether these ideas are accurate it is hard to know. But the nationalists could have seen Jesus as a potential ally. When Jesus cleansed the Temple of merchants and money changers, some of the Zealots may have felt that Jesus was attempting to raise a rebellion. When he did not follow through with their hoped-for armed conflict, the nationalists lost confidence in him as the military Messiah.

Another party was the group called the Herodians. They believed in attempting to seek some sort of semi-autonomous state with the Herod family in control. The party wanted to seek some accommodation with Rome. A good example of this would be Herod Agrippa and his party, which hoped to recreate the kingdom of Herod the Great. Originally started with Herod the Great, the Herodians were often seen by the local Jews as collaborators, since they allowed this non-Jew or semi-Jew to sit on the throne. From their point of view the Herodians wanted to promote Jewish semi-independence. Under Herod the Great Judea existed at its highest point since the time of the Maccabees. But after Herod's death the Jewish state was broken up into several smaller territories ruled by his sons. The region of Judea, however, was soon occupied by the Romans at the request of the Jewish leaders.

The Herodians in Galilee, which was controlled by Herod Antipas, attempted to maintain peace, which allowed them some degree of autonomy. As long as they did not promote too much independence or allow civil unrest to occur, Galilee could maintain some freedom from Roman intrusion. In the 40s C.E. the entire region was reunited under the rule of Herod Agrippa, who had the favor of the emperors Caligula and Claudius. It appears that he attempted not only to bring the entire region under his control, but even to augment his kingdom to create a power in the East. When he died unexpectedly his kingdom was broken up and Rome took over again. The Herodians would ultimately be eliminated during the Great Jewish War. The Herodians viewed Jesus with distrust. As a supposed relative of John the Baptist, who had attacked Herod Antipas for his marriage to his brother's ex-wife, Jesus was viewed with suspicion and was not to be trusted. The Gospels relate how the Herodians attempted to trap Jesus and were aligned with the Pharisees (Matt. 22:15–16; Mark 3:6).

The Sadducees also could be considered a political party. Their political philosophy was based on the aspect of holding the power of the high priesthood. Josephus related that although their numbers were few, their power reached the elites and those who held control. To accomplish this task they were willing to align themselves with the Romans. Their main political base was confined to Jerusalem, because of the temple, and the Pharisees held sway in the outlying areas. To augment the position of the high priest, the Sadducees also heavily influenced the Sanhedrin. This body was more than just the religious court that convicted Jesus; it was the general council that oversaw the Jewish state, working both within and alongside the Roman occupation force. The Sadducees ultimately backed the Zealots in the attempt to throw off the Roman occupation, which led to the Great Jewish War. To the Sadducees and Sanhedrin, Jesus was a potentially dangerous fool who might encourage the masses to rebel and bring the Romans down on the state, as had happened during the period of Quirinius in 6 C.E. To prevent this act the Jewish leaders brought Jesus before the Sanhedrin and ultimately the Romans, accusing him of treason.

ROMAN LEADERS

When Rome took over Judea in 6 C.E. it stumbled into a political hornets' nest. Not understanding the Jewish religion and its penchant for militant reactions, the Romans attempted to rule as they did in other provinces. This, of course, did not work and forced Rome to have a contentious relationship with Judea during the first century C.E. Rome usually dealt with the Jews in a harsh manner, a common Roman strategy. With the destruction of Jerusalem and the later crushing of the rebellion under Hadrian, the Romans effectively eliminated the political power of the Jews. The Romans were arrogant, which did not help the situation. How the Romans viewed Jesus is difficult to say. The Gospels portray Pontius Pilate, the governor who ordered Jesus to be executed, as sympathetic, washing his hands of the whole affair after trying to set Jesus free (Matt. 27:24). This is probably an exaggeration. If anything Pilate probably did not even care; Jesus was simply another potential rebel. If the Jews wanted to execute one of their own rebels then so be it. The story of Pilate releasing the prisoner Barabbas, a dangerous murderer, instead of Jesus, is also probably untrue. The Romans would have seen Jesus as a potential threat because he advocated a new kingdom, or they would have regarded him merely as a troublemaker.

SOCIAL ELITES

Those who had enormous wealth and power often had a different point of view than others. Unlike the poor, who desired a change in government or conditions, the wealthy and powerful desired to ensure that their status remained. Any change would have been potentially dangerous. Jesus clearly had distaste for the wealthy. In the Gospels Jesus constantly berated the wealthy. Statements recorded in the New Testament, such as "It is easier for a camel to enter through the eye of the needle than for a wealthy man to enter heaven," or "What does it profit a man to posses the whole world but lose his soul," point to Jesus having issues with the wealthy (Mark 10: 23–30; Luke 21:1). It appears that none of his immediate disciples were from the social elite. With this negative outlook it is easy to see why wealthy individuals who were the social elite did not support Jesus. Given their close connection with the Sadducees, the social elites distrusted Jesus.

MIDDLE CLASS

The middle class presents some different issues. While Jesus was against the wealthy, or at least viewed them with distrust, it is clear that he was willing to accept middle-class people into his circle. In several passages Jesus is recorded as being at the house of a merchant or conversing with merchants openly. One of his followers was Joseph of Arimathea, who at Jesus' death placed him in his own tomb, indicating his wealth (Matt. 27:57–60; Luke 24:50–56; John 19:38–42). The middle class typically desired to increase their position in society. Some undoubtedly wanted to increase their position by trade or marriage, to enter into a higher social class. To accomplish this they would often provide beneficence to their city or fellow citizens. For example, they would provide grain or wine, games, races, or parties for their fellow citizens. While it is not clear how many followed Jesus, some must have worried that he would upset the balance that existed and potentially damage their chances to move ahead.

COMMON PEOPLE

The poor or common people were not just one group; rather they were a mixture of different sections of society. Some did not care about politics, while others would gladly follow someone who promised them more. There were competing views expressed by individuals attempting to garner support. This is shown in the Gospels when the followers of John the Baptist appear to clash with Jesus' group, even though they may have had similar messages. Jesus clearly had the poor in mind. For example, in the Beatitudes Jesus praises the poor; by attacking the rich Jesus implicitly supported the poor (Luke 6:20). The common man could still turn into the mob. In the Gospels Jesus was praised on Sunday and railed against on Friday. But the reason for this change had to do with the fact that the common people expected different images of the Messiah. Some wanted a military and political leader. When Jesus made it clear that he was not going to be a military or political leader, this segment of the masses abandoned him. When Jesus did not provide the poor with immediate riches they in turn walked away from him. Those that did continue to support Jesus probably were presented with alternate points. For example, some alternate views would be that Rome would ultimately leave, or that the

Jewish leaders would ensure that the poor were taken care of. These competing views influenced the masses, and some who had supported Jesus may have left.

CHILDREN

Throughout the Gospels children are extolled and favored by Jesus (Mark 10:13–16, 23–24; Luke 9:46–47). In some passages Jesus reminds his disciples that they are to be like children. The implication is that they were to be innocent and open to receiving his message. When children approached him and his disciples attempted to prevent them from coming near him, Jesus chastised them and let them come near. His popularity with children must have been phenomenal and clearly showed his connection with them. It is clear from the Gospels that they admired and liked him. While they did not have immediate power, they nevertheless were the future of Judaism and later Christianity. It would be easy to imagine that some of these children remained loyal to his message and became Christians during that crucial early period from the 40s to 70 C.E. when Christianity was differentiating itself from Judaism.

NON-JEWS IN PALESTINE

The region of Palestine contained other groups, but these were non-Jewish ethnic and religious groups. One such group was the Samaritans. Although the Romans probably saw them as Jewish, they had separated themselves from Judaism and set themselves up as the true successors of Moses. The animosity between the Samaritans and Jews was legendary, with neither side wishing to associate with the others. While there was animosity, Jesus appears not to have suffered from the racism. In one passage Jesus asks a Samaritan woman for water and they converse. She then goes into her town and tells everyone about Jesus and his powers; they in turn come out and listen to him and believe in him (John 4:16–18). Although this was only one story, and perhaps an allegory, our sources do not show much hostility. Granted, the number of sources is small.

Other non-Jews existed along the shoreline of the Mediterranean Sea, in places like Tyre and Sidon. These ancient Phoenician cities were renowned for their trade. Jesus visited them at least once and preached there. Their view of Jesus was either noncommittal or positive. There does not appear to have been any great hostility between Jesus and his disciples and the citizens of these cities.

INDIVIDUALS OUTSIDE PALESTINE

Individuals residing outside of Palestine during the time of Jesus probably did not know him. However, due to Paul's missionary activities, Jesus, or at least his message, later became available to others. When Paul and the other early missionaries arrived in towns they first went to the homes of Jews, taught in synagogues, and tried to convert them. If they were received they then attempted to bring in non-Jews, known to the Jews as gentiles. Often the local Jews were against them and the missionaries preached to the gentiles. This resulted in the advance of Christianity. Within a short time the Christian gentiles outnumbered the Christian Jews, resulting in a large difference in populations. This difference led not only to some violence between the groups but to the ultimate split between Judaism and Christianity. At this point the normal Jewish holidays and feast days were often transposed to other days or altered. For example, the traditional Jewish worship day of the Sabbath (Saturday) was now moved to Sunday. How did these people view Jesus? Clearly the gentiles who believed in Jesus viewed him as the Messiah or savior; the non-Christian gentiles at this time probably did not have much of an opinion, but within a half-century there would be violence between the two; for the Jews who did not follow Jesus there was distrust and often violence.

WHO WAS JESUS?

Historically Jesus existed. He is mentioned not only in the New Testament, but in Jewish sources such as Josephus and the Talmud, and in non-Jewish sources. But answers to questions concerning his birth, parentage, place of origin, early childhood, and family life are all disputed and fragmentary. In the New Testament there are two stories concerning his birth. Matthew records that Jesus was born during the reign of Herod (Matt. 2:1–12). Because he later mentions his son Archelaus as king, the assumption is that the Herod mentioned is Herod the Great. Historically Herod died in 4 B.C.E., indicating that Jesus must have been born before this time, but just when is not clear. Luke mentions that Jesus was born during the reign of the Emperor Augustus when Quirinius was governor of Syria, which began in 6 C.E (Luke 2:1–7). This of course leads to a difficulty: if one believes Matthew Jesus was born around 6 B.C.E., but if one believes Luke, after 6 C.E., a variance of 10–12 years. However, it is known that Quirinius was previously military governor of Pamphylia-Galatia in 6 B.C.E. before becoming governor of Syria in 6 C.E., and it may be that Luke had his first governorship in mind when he declared he was governor of Syria. This mistake would have been easily understandable because he was known to have been governor twice over, just not in the same region.

Luke further complicates the issue when he declares that John the Baptist preached during the 15th year of the reign of Tiberius, 29 C.E., and that Jesus began his ministry soon after when he was about 30 years old (Luke 3:1–3, 21–23). If this was true then Jesus would have been born around 2 B.C.E., after the death of Herod the Great, when Quirinius was still in the

254 Site of Christ's Baptism at the Jordan.

Site of Christ's baptism at the Jordan River. Courtesy of
Library of Congress.

east as military advisor to Gaius, Augustus's grandson. Of course Jesus
could still have been born before 4 B.C.E and be about 30 when he began
his ministry. Luke also records that at the age of 12 he went to Jerusalem
with his family for the great festival, presumably Passover, and remained
behind while his parents returned home (Luke 2:41–51). This was the last
reference to Joseph, Jesus' father, and when Luke records Jesus' ministry
Joseph is not mentioned. Jesus' family life is not mentioned much in any
of the sources.

The Gospels concentrate on his ministry and the message that he attempted to bring. But the Gospels also need to be seen not as historical
works or biographies, but rather as a message about his divinity. Each of
the Gospels had a different audience. Mark was probably written first,
seemingly in the late 60s C.E. Although written for a Greek audience,
probably in Greek, because he explains Aramaic terms, he may have had
in mind the Jews living in the Diaspora who knew only Greek and did
not have direct ties with Palestine. Matthew's Gospel was probably written in the 70s or early 80s and borrowed from Mark's. Some believe that
Matthew's Gospel may have been written earlier than Mark's, but this is
not the view of the majority of scholars. Written in Greek, it was probably

addressed to the Jews and seems to have been based in Jewish traditions. The work was probably for the Jewish Christians. The Gospel of Luke was written in Greek during the 80s and 90s. The same author wrote the Acts of the Apostles, and Luke is the only Gospel that seems to be a historical account with a selected methodology. The Gospel appears to have been written for the non-Jews, the gentiles. As such this Gospel attempted to explain Jesus and his position in monotheistic Judaism to the gentiles. These three Gospels, known as the Synoptic Gospels, show similarity in their message and plan. The final Gospel, John's, was written to show the reader that Jesus was the Messiah, the chosen one. His Gospel is theological and is meant to show the *logos*, or the word of God. The Gospel appears to have been written in the late 90s and was probably the last of the Gospels written.

The life of Jesus as related in the Gospels is incomplete. We do not know what he truly believed about certain issues. The account of the ministry of Jesus is not even secure, because the chronology and geography of each of the Gospels are often at odds with one another. Since the Gospels are not really meant to be full biographies, we should not criticize them too much. The central theme of all of the Gospels was Jesus' passion, death, and resurrection.

It is clear from all of the Gospels that Jesus was betrayed by one of his own disciples, Judas Iscariot (Matt. 26:47–56; Luke 22:47–53). The reason for the betrayal is not given; it could have been that Judas felt that Jesus was not living up to Judas's expectations, or that Jesus had lost the respect of the crowd, or that Judas was simply afraid. Regardless of the reason Jesus was betrayed and arrested, his trial before the Jewish authorities rested upon his claim of divinity. To the Jewish leadership Jesus had committed heresy. The Jewish court, however, appears not to have had the authority to pass a capital sentence. The Roman governor Pontius Pilate attempted to pawn Jesus off to Herod Antipas on the grounds that Jesus came from Galilee, Herod's province. Ultimately Jesus was condemned to death by Pilate and was then crucified. Crucifixion was the standard punishment for slaves, rebels, and the lower social classes, with the condemned often living for several days before dying of drowning from the pressure exerted upon the lungs. Jesus' quick death, because he was probably already abused from sleep deprivation and being whipped, resulted in his not having his legs broken, like his fellow condemned prisoners. After his death Jesus was laid in a nearby tomb. Practice would have had it that after his body decomposed his bones would then have been put into an ossuary, a stone box that would have provided his final resting place. For the followers of Jesus this was not needed because he arose from the dead. The Gospels in the New Testament are referred to as the canonical Gospels, which were recognized by the early Christian communities as works confirmed by God and inspired by God. These were not the only works that referred to Jesus, as others existed that influenced the early history of Christianity.

OTHER WORKS

The New Testament contains works other than the Gospels. The Acts of the Apostles, written by the same author as the Gospel of Luke, describes the early history of the Christians. The first section relates the ministry of the disciples of Jesus, most notably Peter. The second relates the ministry of Paul. Other works in the New Testament are the letters of Paul, James, Peter, John, and Jude, and the Apocalypse (Revelation). These works discuss issues that were of importance to the early Church.

Two early works that are not part of the canonical tradition are the Gospel of Thomas and the Gospel of Peter. The Gospel of Thomas is known through the Nag Hammadi texts (discovered in Egypt in the twentieth century) and is a Coptic translation of an earlier work. Some authors argue that it was written in the first century C.E. and that it should be seen as a canonical source. The argument is that Thomas differed from John's Gospel theologically. Tradition holds that the work, a product of the Gnostic community, was banned by most Christian communities because it argued against the ideas of the other Gospels. The Gospel of Peter was a narrative that discussed the passion of Jesus. This text, which is now only preserved incompletely, relates that Herod Antipas and not Pilate was responsible for Jesus' death. The work gives more details to the events after Jesus' death, his entombment, and his resurrection and ascension (which occur on the same day in this source). These two works then present information and ideas that are outside the canonical texts. Why were they not accepted? There are several probable reasons. They may not have been known, at least fully, by the early Church. They may have been known and deemed heretical. They may have been written after the formation of the canonical texts. Regardless of the reason for their omission, they do present more information that helps supplement the New Testament Gospels.

Other works of importance included the Didache, an early second-century manual written to instruct converts, originally a compilation of four parts: the two ways; rituals for fasting, baptism, and communion; dealing with traveling prophets; and an apocalypse. The Epistle of Barnabas, written after the destruction of the Temple and before the Bar Kochba rebellion (a Jewish revolt in 132 C.E.), probably to Christian gentiles, may have sought an accommodation between the gentiles and Jewish Christians. There were two letters ascribed to be from Clement, pope in Rome. Although not canonical, the letters were still revered by the early Church; the letters were addressed to the church in Corinth to help settle a dispute. The Shepherd of Hermes, written around 100–150, was considered canonical for several centuries before being excluded. The work, supposedly written by a slave, contains five visions, commandments, and parables. Other works included the Gospel of Judas, Infancy of Jesus, and Apocalypse of Peter, which were Gnostic works. These works attempted to explain the message of Jesus to those who knew the secrets. The Gnostic works centered on the idea of dualism, the struggle between good and evil. Part of their ritual was ascetic living, seen best in the practice of ritual fasting and abstinence. These works are seen as Apocrypha, and their authorship is uncertain. Many of the texts claim to have been written by early church officials, including some of the original apostles, although in reality they were written well after the first century. Some of these texts have value in understanding the formation of the early Church while others were merely spurious.

DAILY LIFE

During the first century C.E. the region of the New Testament underwent tremendous changes, not only in the religious but in the political, social, and economic spheres. The main religion of Judea, Judaism, was not a homogenous philosophy. The religion had three to four major sects at the time of Jesus' birth. Each one operated under the general guise of Judaism but had distinct differences; the Pharisees believed in the resurrection of the body while the Sadducees did not. The Zealots argued for a violent response against the Romans while the Essenes wanted to remove themselves from society. Into this mix entered Jesus, who taught a variety of different Jewish views, liberal, conservative, and revolutionary. The region likewise changed politically during the time of Jesus. At the time of his birth Judea and Galilee were ruled by Herod, at the time of his death Judea was under Roman control, and within a generation Jerusalem had been destroyed and Palestine was under military occupation by Rome. These changes made the daily life of individuals different in each period. The social environment also changed during the first century C.E. Avenues were open for advancement for many parts of society. The region saw an influx of Roman veterans, who often became the new social elites. With more stability after the Roman civil wars, society became more fluid. These changes also allowed for economic stimulation for the region. With changes in society and politics, individuals could now become more innovative. Merchants were able to move their products without political barriers. All of these factors influenced the daily lives of inhabitants in Palestine.

Daily life during New Testament times was not confined to the region of Palestine. The missionary activities of Paul took the new faith, Christianity, to non-Jewish lands, mainly Asia Minor and Greece. With the spread of Christianity into these Hellenistic regions, Christianity transformed itself, and with this so did the people's daily life. The first century C.E. was a period of intense change. With the consolidation of the emperor's power, the creation of an empire, the transformation of the Mediterranean region into an economically unified region, and the opening of the social ranks, there existed a whole range of possibilities for change. For individuals interested in exploring their philosophical outlook, the first century held immense opportunities. With changes in religious outlooks and philosophies, daily life also changed.

This book attempts to set the stage for understanding daily life during the New Testament period, mainly in Palestine. The various chapters on the geography and history of the region, the different ethnic groups in the region, and nonreligious factors that heavily influenced daily life will be examined. The next segment examines pre-messianic Judaism and the expectations for the Messiah. The various occupations, and daily life of peasants and individuals complete the picture. The final section explores Rome and its occupation and the lasting impact of its daily life on the modern world.

NOTE

1. Harry Fosdick, *The Man from Nazareth* (New York: Harper and Brothers, 1949), 194.

CHRONOLOGY

323 B.C.E.	Death of Alexander the Great.
174–163	Antiochus IV Epiphanes attempts to Hellenize Palestine.
168–142	Maccabee rebellion.
140–137	The Hasmonean Kingdom.
134–104	John Hyrcanus forcibly extends Judaism into Galilee and Idumeans.
63	Roman General Pompey captures Jerusalem and plunders the Temple.
40	Roman Senate, under the direction of Mark Antony, appoints Herod King of the Jews and gives him command over Judea, Samaria, and Galilee.
6–4	Jesus and John the Baptist born.
4	Death of Herod the Great.
4 B.C.E.**–39** C.E.	Herod Antipas (son of Herod the Great) rules as tetrarch over Galilee.
4 B.C.E**–6** C.E.	Herod Archelaus (son of Herod the Great) rules as ethnarch over Judea until deposed.

6 C.E.	Judea becomes a Roman province; Quirinius, governor of Syria, conducts a census that leads to the rebellion by Judas of Galilee, which Quirinius suppresses. Procurator (governor) controls only Judea.
7–9	Coponius, first procurator (governor) of Judea.
9–12	Marcus Ambibulus procurator.
12–15	Annius Rufus procurator.
15–26	Valerius Gratus procurator, appoints Annas as High Priest.
6–26	Period of peace.
9	Hillel the Elder dies.
18–36	Caiaphas made High Priest by the procurator Gratus, removed by governor of Syria, Vitellius.
26–36	Pontius Pilate, governor, deposed by Vitellius; Marcellus acts as Vitellius' agent, probably not procurator during 36–37.
29–30	Ministry and death of John of Baptist, ministry and death of Jesus.
37–41	Marulus procurator.
40	Paul converted.
41–44	Herod Agrippa appointed King of the Jews by Claudius.
42	James, Apostle of Jesus and head of Christian Church in Jerusalem, executed.
44–46	Following death of Herod, Judea, Samaria, and Gallilee under procurator's control, Cuspius Fadus procurator.
46–48	Tiberius Alexander, who was born Jewish, is made procurator in hopes of preventing discord.
47–67	Paul's missionary.
48–52	Ventidius Cumanus, procurator known for his harshness, removed by request of Jewish officials.
52–60	Felix made procurator at the request of the Jewish High Priest, oversaw initial investigation of Paul.
60–62	Porcius Festus, procurator, examines the case against Paul. Known for his fairness, he arrives too late to prevent the upcoming rebellion, dies in office.

62–64	Albinus, procurator, known for his extortions against the locals.
63–66	Gessius Florus, procurator, his actions result in the Jewish rebellion.
	First Jewish rebellion.
	Vespasian captures the north of Israel.
67	Paul and Peter executed.
69	Vespasian proclaimed emperor, his son Titus takes over command.
70	Titus captures Jerusalem and the Temple is burned.
73	General Silva captures the Jewish stronghold Masada and finds all of the inhabitants dead.
91–95	Domitian persecutes Jews and Christians.
132–135	Second Jewish rebellion, Bar Kokhba revolt, Romans rename Jerusalem Aelia Capitolia during reign of Hadrian.

1

GEOGRAPHICAL AND HISTORICAL OVERVIEW

A certain man went down from Jerusalem to Jericho, and fell among thieves, who stripped him of his clothing, wounded him and departed, leaving him half dead....But a certain Samaritan, as he journeyed, came where he was...and he set him on his own animal, brought him to an inn, and took care of him. On the next day, when he departed, he took out two *denarii*, gave them to the innkeeper, and said to him, Take care of him; and whatever more you spend, when I come again, I will repay you. (Luke 10:30–35)

The opening statement to the parable captures the geographic situation of Judea in the time of the New Testament. While it may seem rather innocuous, the statement in fact contains a vivid account of space and direction. Jericho, lying on one of the major roads to Jerusalem, was about 15 miles from Jerusalem and about 1,500 feet below it in elevation. When Jesus began his parable, those listening would automatically have in their mind an idea of what kind of terrain, distance, and effort the traveler faced. The parable then continued by stating that the traveler was attacked by robbers. Again, for Jesus' listeners, the image would have been common. Judea had a history of problems with highway robbers. The image would not have been hard to grasp. Jesus could have easily substituted "soldiers" or "extremists (Zealots)" for "robbers" and the point would have been just as dramatic. The parable continues with a Pharisee and Sadducee passing the wounded man without providing aid. For Jesus' audience the two major religious groups would have been well known. Finally the parable ends with a passing Samaritan merchant helping the traveler, taking him to an inn, and promising the owner that upon his return he would make up any extra cost. This part of the parable joined the religious act of charity, long a hallmark of Judaism, with the religious sectarianism between Jews and Samaritans, in a geographical setting.

GEOGRAPHY OF THE NEW TESTAMENT

Geography and history are often intertwined in the history of a nation or people, even in their daily life. This is especially true for the region of the eastern Mediterranean traditionally called Palestine. The daily life of individuals depicted in the New Testament clearly shows the influence of geography and history. Passages in the New Testament relate to regions such as Galilee, Samaria, and Judea inside Palestine, along with Cyprus, Greece, Asia Minor, and Italy outside. This chapter will explore the interaction and description of history and geography, especially in Palestine, as it relates to the New Testament.

PALESTINE

The overall geographical region in the Mideast is that of Palestine. Although in many ways an artificial creation without any real ethnic, geographical, or national position, Palestine is recognized and familiar to most people. Encompassing parts of the modern region of Lebanon, Israel, Egypt (Sinai Peninsula), and Syria, the term *Palestine* can be used as a general frame for discussing the ancient regions mentioned in the New Testament. More specific, but fluid, regions existed. These include Galilee, Samaria, Judea, Peraea, and Idumaea. These are the regions in which Jesus and his contemporaries traveled or with which they were familiar. The geography of the region can be divided into a series of parallel highlands and valleys moving away from the Mediterranean. For example, the Jordan River begins in Galilee at Lake Huleh, which is seven feet above sea level. It travels 10 miles to the Sea (actually a lake) of Galilee, which is 685 feet below sea level. The river then moves 65 miles more to the Dead Sea, which is 1,290 feet below sea level, after which the land rises to 300 feet above sea level before dropping slowly to the Gulf of Akabah and the Red Sea.

The Jordan River valley is only one of a series of rifts. Moving from the Mediterranean Sea to the desert there are a series of these parallel lines. First is the Maritime Plain, which is only 6 miles wide in the north but broadens out to 30 miles in the south. It is the most fertile part of Judea. This region is influenced by the sea, both in climate, which is nearly tropical; and commercially, because there are few ports and no natural harbors in this region because the silt of the Nile River flowing counterclockwise

View of the Jordan River and its surroundings from top of hill, Palestine. Courtesy of Library of Congress.

has silted up the harbor of Joppa (Jaffa) and Tyre's southern harbor. Herod built the port of Caesarea Maritime, which allowed the region to receive and send goods to all corners of the Mediterranean. The next line is the Central Range, or the Western Syrian Ridge, a long deep wall of limestone running from Lebanon to the Red Sea, broken up with valleys and ridges. It is on this range that the city of Jerusalem sits. The land is broken up into small regions or units, with temperature extremes (over 100 degrees in the summer), and where the flow of water is unequal. The Jordan River valley follows next with the Eastern Syrian Range, more continuous than the Central or Western Ridge. It starts from Mt. Hermon at 2,000 feet above sea level and runs down to the Red Sea at an almost constant level. Finally, the desert of Arabia begins an inhospitable land. The lands of Palestine had a varied fauna, with pastures, woodlands, brush lands, fruit trees, olives groves, vineyards, and, on the lower plateaus, grain land. The region is harsh; however, traveling from Jerusalem east through Jericho to the Dead Sea the land drops nearly 4,000 feet in 15 miles. There is no source of water from Jericho up to Jerusalem until one arrives at the Mount of Olives.

The entire region is relatively small, only about 6,000 square miles. In the north in the Plain of Esdraelon lies the Valley of Megiddo (Armageddon) in the west and the Valley of Jezreel in the east, while the hills of Galilee on the north and the hills of Ephraim and Judah on the south control entrance into Israel. Whoever controlled this region controlled the key to Palestine and its resources. Esdraelon is the most fertile region here, and it became and has remained of major importance. From the land of Dan in the north, 150 miles south to Beersheba is the entire land of Israel. The Jordan, only 65 miles long, is 28 miles from the coast in the north and the Dead Sea is 54 miles from the coast in the south. Elevation changes are also pronounced. Mt. Hermon in the north is 9,200 feet above sea level, while the Dead Sea is 1,275 feet below, a range of 10,475 feet in less than 100 miles.

These geographical regions also show the religious differences in Judaism. Judea was the original heartland for Judaism, but other regions had received Judaism as well. To the north Samaria put forward a claim to counter Judea's traditional hold on the Temple and its organization. Further north, Galilee had recently (100 B.C.E.) converted to Judaism, although Jews from Judea considered them inferior. The hold of Jerusalem and the Temple, however, brought Jews to Judea, giving many of them a sense of community.

There were also pockets of Jews outside Palestine who influenced life in the era described in the New Testament. There was a large Jewish population in Babylon, descendents of those who were exiled in 587 B.C.E. and did not return after the fall of Babylon. A large number lived in Alexandria, Egypt, descendents of colonists who migrated there during the reign of the Ptolemies, successors of Alexander the Great (356–333 B.C.E.). In Asia Minor, in many of the cities such as Ephesus, Antioch, and Tarsus, Jewish settlers had arrived during the reign of the Seleucids, another kingdom established by one of Alexander's successors. Jews also lived in Greece and Italy, having migrated to many of the cities during the late Roman Republic. Judaism had become more cosmopolitan during the two centuries before Jesus.

JEWISH HISTORY

This interconnection between the different Jewish groups was a product of history. The Jewish kingdom, united under David and Solomon, split into a northern kingdom, Israel, and a southern kingdom, Judah. Israel fell to the Assyrians in the eighth century B.C.E., with many of its inhabitants enslaved and transplanted into the Assyrian interior. Judah held out for another century but ultimately fell in 587 to Nebuchadnezzar of Babylon, a city that had recently destroyed the Assyrian power. The Babylonians deported many of the leading families to Babylon as hostages, but a sizeable contingent remained in Judea. After 70 years the captivity ended with the conquest of the region by Persia under Cyrus the Great. The Jews were allowed to return to Judea, although many remained in Babylon, and were given aid by Persia to rebuild the Temple. The returning Jews created some hostilities with the indigenous residents. Disagreements—often hostile—also erupted with inhabitants of the former northern kingdom, known as Samaritans, who were seen as impure because the area had been populated by foreigners.

Alexander's conquest of Persia brought in a new political and cultural group, the Macedonian Greeks. As outside conquerors the Macedonians did not have a shared history of the region, and the gulf between the Jews and the Macedonians resulted not only in a political upheaval but in a cultural/religious war. Initially the region of Judea was controlled by the Ptolemies in Egypt, beginning in 323 B.C.E. The country was not ruled by a governor appointed by Alexandria but was self-governed by the Jewish Council of Elders with a high priest as chairman of the council. To ensure that the Jews did not create too much trouble, the Ptolemies founded a series of Greco-Macedonian settlements around Judea. These colonists not only ensured that the Jews would not rebel, but they also imported their own religion and philosophy, which challenged Judaism. The Jews had been forced throughout their history to challenge other religious practices by their Semitic neighbors, but now they had to further cope with Hellenism and its pagan philosophy, supported by the monarchy in Egypt.

The Ptolemaic capital Alexandria became the center for the Eastern Mediterranean. Jews who had resided in Egypt already now flocked to Alexandria, which became the largest center outside Palestine. The Jews were allowed to practice their religion in the city, and the oldest known synagogue was located only 14 miles away at Schedia. Anti-Semitism, not entirely unknown, now increased, often leading to violent clashes. To counter the works by Greeks in the city, the Jews translated the Bible from Hebrew into Greek. This translation was known as the *Septuagint,* or "seventy," supposedly meaning that the work was done by 70 translators. Although the text was to provide the pagan Greeks with the Jewish Bible and ideally lead to a better understanding of the Jews by the Greeks, it probably did not succeed. Most of the Greeks would not have understood the stories and prophecies, because Judaism centered on the belief in one God, something alien to the Greeks. What the Septuagint did do, however, was give the Jewish community in Alexandria, and ultimately elsewhere, a Bible that they could understand, because most did not know Hebrew.

Palestine, however, continued to be seen as the gateway to Egypt and Syria. This unique position led to continual hostilities between Ptolemaic Egypt and the Seleucids in Syria. The third century B.C.E. witnessed continual conflicts for control of Palestine. The Ptolemies were forced to recruit more and more mercenaries, especially from the Idumaeans, descendents of the Edomites. In 200 the Seleucid Antiochus III defeated the Ptolemies and now controlled the region. Many in Judea welcomed the takeover because they still had connections with Babylon. Antiochus allowed the Jews to control the internal workings of the state through the high priest and the Council of Elders. The Temple was not taxed and the state flourished. Soon the situation changed. Taxation increased dramatically until within 25 years the land tax amounted to nearly one-third of the produce, and the Temple itself was either plundered or nearly plundered under Seleucus IV (187–175). The rise in taxes was caused by the Seleucids' requirement to pay tribute to Rome after losing control to them in 189 B.C.E.

These upheavals caused a split in and among the leading Jewish families. Some desired to return to the Ptolemies and eject the Seleucids, while others desired to remain under Seleucid control. The prize in each camp was control of the high priesthood and its influence over the council. The Tobaid family, who controlled the high priesthood, was split. This split was not only political but also cultural. The pro-Seleucid side was more Hellenized, more accepting of Greek culture. In 180 the high priest Onias III was probably pro-Ptolemaic while his brother Jason (Joshua, Jesus) was pro-Seleucid. Jason paid Antiochus IV Epiphanes (175–163) to become high priest in place of his brother. Jason began to convert Jerusalem into a Greek city coexisting beside a Jewish city. The Greek section contained a gymnasium where uncircumcised men performed in the nude, a shock to most Jews. In 175 Jason was overthrown and replaced by Menelaus, a more ardent pro-Hellenizer who promised Antiochus IV Temple gold and allowed a Seleucid garrison into the city. Jason returned, imprisoned Menelaus, ended his earlier attempt to create a Greek city, and expelled the Seleucid garrison. Antiochus, who was fighting the Ptolemies and Parthians in Iran, seized Jerusalem, pulled down its walls, looted the treasury, fortified the citadel with a new garrison, and reinstalled Menelaus. Antiochus further punished the Jews by forbidding circumcision and celebrations of the Sabbath. Antiochus additionally ordered official sacrifice for the pagan gods and in 167 he formally rededicated the Jewish Temple as a shrine to Zeus.

Although Antiochus had attempted to merge the worship of other gods under the general guise of Zeus, represented by Antiochus himself, he had never sought to annihilate a religion before. His actions against the Jews went beyond the syncretism of religions and should be seen as outright hostility. The result of Antiochus's policy was open rebellion, the Maccabean Revolt, named after the family leading the revolt. They were also known as Hasmonaeans and belonged to the priestly clan of Joarib but were not from the house of Zadok, the clan that had traditionally controlled the high priesthood.

Mattathias started the rebellion by not offering sacrifice and killing a fellow Jew who had complied. To escape punishment, Mattathias and his five sons, together with others, fled into the mountains. Most of those who fled were from the poorer elements of society, and it soon became a rebellion centered on class. After Mattathias's death in 166, his son Judas

Maccabaeus became leader of the guerrilla war. In 164 Judas success-fully retook Jerusalem and the Temple was re-consecrated, celebrated by the Festival of Lights (Hanukkah) using a seven-branched candelabrum, the Menorah. Judas, knowing that he needed help to resist the Seleu-cids, made a treaty with Rome (160 B.C.E.) and renewed it 20 years later. Rome gladly helped the Jewish state, because it allowed them presence in the Seleucid backyard to continually keep an eye on them. Judas died in battle in 160 and was succeeded by his brother Jonathan. Judas had not become high priest because he was not from the house of Aaron, but Jona-than allowed himself to be proclaimed not only the secular leader but the religious leader (high priest) as well. He successfully took Joppa on the Mediterranean but also secured Seleucid recognition as governor of Judea after giving them military aid. Like his brother, he died in battle. Simon, the last surviving son of Mattathias, expelled the Seleucid garrison from Jerusalem, captured the fortress at Gazara (Gezer), and forced the Seleu-cid king to recognize Judea as independent. Simon became high priest and styled himself as *ethnarch,* a term denoting ruler of an *ethnos* (nation), but not quite king.

For the next 80 years Judea was an independent nation, except for a brief Seleucid period of control from 135–129 B.C.E. Simon was assas-sinated in 135, leading to Antiochus VII Sidetes's reconquest of Judea, which lasted until his death in 129. Simon's son John Hyrcanus I (134–104) renewed the treaty with Rome, guaranteeing the Jewish state's indepen-dence from both Ptolemaic Egypt and Seleucid Syria. It was under his rule that the areas of Samaria, Galilee, and Idumaea were annexed. He pun-ished the Samaritans for not supporting the Maccabean revolt by destroy-ing their temple on Mount Gerizim and the Hellenized town of Samaria. In Galilee, where some missionary activity had already taken place, John Hyrcanus now forcibly converted the remainder; his control and conver-sion of Galilee would mean that it had only been Jewish for only 100 years when Jesus was born and preached. John Hyrcanus also forced the inhab-itants of Idumaea to undergo circumcision and accept Judaism. The Phari-sees did not believe that these conversions were valid because they had been forced upon the inhabitants. John Hyrcanus was succeeded by his sons Aristobulus (104–103) and Alexander Jannaeus (103–76), who now as-sumed the title of king. Alexander conquered the southern region around Gaza, defeating the Nabataeans, and he exerted control over the Judean coastline, punishing the Greek cities. Some Pharisees revolted against Alexander, probably because of the reduction in power of the Council of Elders and the idea that a monarch could not be high priest. Alexander crushed the rebellion and executed hundreds of Pharisees. His widow Salome Alexander succeeded him (76–67). She reversed his religious pol-icy and favored the Pharisees who, together with their allies, the Scribes, controlled the Great Sanhedrin and countered the Sadducees. Her eldest son, John Hyrcanus II, was made high priest and ruled after her death.

His chief advisor, Antipater from Idumaea, became the real power behind the throne. In 63 B.C.E. the entire eastern Mediterranean's political front changed when Pompey the Great from Rome arrived.

Pompey had been given command to deal with pirates, and upon completion of this task decided to reorganize and reshape the political landscape in the east. Pompey ended the Seleucid power and annexed Syria, bringing Rome into direct contact with Judea. John Hyrcanus II and his brother Aristobulus II, who were engaged in a power struggle, both approached Pompey, who gave Aristobulus control. Aristobulus, however, did not provide Pompey with the necessary provisions of money and support and was removed and replaced by John Hyrcanus. Pompey also seized Jerusalem and entered the Temple's Holy of Holies, committing in the eyes of the Jews a blasphemy and desecration. John Hyrcanus remained as chief priest, but his territory was reduced to Judea and Galilee, but not Samaria, and he received the title of ethnarch. A few years later John Hyrcanus was deprived of the title but still retained title of chief priest and controlled the city of Jerusalem, and his domains were carved up into five separate units controlled by the Sadducees. Antipater, who collaborated with the Romans, was given control of his native Idumaea. During the troubled times of the First Triumvirate (Crassus, Pompey, and Caesar) Judea was subject to Roman control, including Crassus's seizure of the Temple treasury. With Caesar's control of Rome after defeating Pompey and John Hyrcanus and Antipater's help in supporting Caesar in Egypt, the Jewish state received its rewards. John Hyrcanus not only received his former territories but was given Joppa and the plain of Jezreel. He also received the title of ethnarch, and Antipater became his chief minister with his sons Phasael controlling Jerusalem and Herod in charge of Galilee. Caesar also extended protection of the Jews in the Greek cities of the Diaspora and exempted them from military service. Although future Romans would continually reaffirm the protection and liberty of Jews in the Greek cities, there was continual tension between the Greeks and Jews.

RULE OF HEROD THE GREAT

With Caesar's assassination (44) and the Parthian attack on Asia Minor (40), Judea was beset with problems. John Hyrcanus was dethroned, Phasael was killed, and Herod fled while John's nephew Antigonus became king. Herod made his way to Rome where he met Antony, one of Caesar's lieutenants, who was currently ruling with Octavian (the future Augustus), Caesar's adopted son. Antony convinced the Roman Senate to make a treaty with Herod recognizing him as king of Judea. The Hasmonaean dynasty of the Maccabees, of Jewish descent, had been overthrown by the Idumaean dynasty of recent converts. Retaking Jerusalem from Antigonus in 37, Herod became ruler of Judea and Samaria but not of the lands near Egypt, which were annexed by Cleopatra. Internally Herod executed 45 of the 71 members of the Sanhedrin who had supported Antigonus, most of whom were Sadducees. The leaders of the Sanhedrin, Hillel and Shammai (both Pharisees), decided to engage in a policy of nonresistance to Herod's rule. The office of the high priest was separated from the secular rule because Herod came from a race and family that could not aspire to become high priest.

After Antony and Cleopatra's defeat by Octavian at Actium, Herod declared his loyalty to Octavian and in return received the bordering areas of his kingdom that Pompey had removed earlier. He executed his wife Mariamne and her mother Alexandra (daughter of John Hyrcanus II) because of an alleged plot against him.

Herod's rule under Augustus (formerly Octavian) produced a period of both prosperity and paranoia in Palestine. In his foreign affairs Herod promoted the Jewish cause by serving Augustus loyally. In addition he behaved as a proper client king. He erected Greco-Roman structures such as a theater and amphitheatre in Jerusalem, made the town of Samaria into a new Greek city renamed Sebaste (Greek for Augustus), and constructed a new port, Caesarea, the best harbor ever seen in Judea. He fortified Judea with palaces/fortresses at Jericho, Herodium, Machaerus, and Masada. He promoted his image in Judaism by rebuilding the Temple in Jerusalem and a new fortress, the Antonia, which allowed Jerusalem to become a center for pilgrims. Jews throughout the Mediterranean flocked to Jerusalem and its new Temple. Herod supported Augustus's policies in the east and was rewarded for that. He received parts of southern Syria, ensuring that the rich Babylonian pilgrim traffic was in his hands, and his brother Pheroras became governor of Peraea, across the Jordan River. He helped his subjects during times of famine and he presented gifts to the Greek cities in the east, securing his appointment as president of the Olympic Games. If this was the only picture of Herod known, our image of him would be that of a great ruler who gave his people peace and prosperity.

Unfortunately, paranoia also existed in Judea, a paranoia caused directly by Herod, who distrusted his family. Herod feared that his sons and other family members were constantly plotting against his life and rule. He executed numerous members of his family, which shocked even Augustus.

Further complicating this issue was Herod's attempt to seize the Nabataean kingdom. This angered Augustus, because the kingdom was also a client of Rome. Not only was the invasion a fiasco, it strained relations with Rome. To appease the emperor, Herod sent his chief advisor Nicolaus of Damascus to plead his case. He did so by arguing that the invasion had been exaggerated and that it was merely a "raid." Herod then ordered his subjects to swear an oath of loyalty to Augustus and himself, which set off a firestorm by many Jews, who viewed it as a step toward worshipping the emperor's statues as in Greek cities. Several of the leading Pharisees refused to sacrifice, and Herod was forced to save face by only fining them. He was further embarrassed when his brother Pheroras paid the fines.

Jewish eschatological teachings had included the arrival of a Messiah, something that evoked fear in Herod, because he believed that only he should be seen as Judaism's savior. When some Pharisees convinced his eunuch Bagoas that he would become the father of the Messiah by some Pharisees, Herod executed him for treason. Herod had placed an eagle on his coins but now proceeded to erect the same image on the main gate of the Temple. The eagle was regarded as a symbol of Rome, and Jewish rioters pulled the image down. Herod, who was in Jericho suffering in his last days, ordered the rioters executed; he also had his eldest son Antipater executed. These incidents, together with the stories about the slaughter of the innocents from Christian writers (Matt. 2:16), further blackened Herod's memory. His death ended the power of Judea and set into place its position during New Testament times.

PALESTINE IN THE TIMES OF THE GOSPELS

Augustus divided Herod's kingdom between three sons; Archelaus ruled over Judea and Samaria as ethnarch, Herod Antipas over the two separate regions of Galilee and Peraea as tetrarch, and Philip over parts of southern Syria, also as tetrarch. After a tumultuous and heavy-handed 10-year rule, Jews and Samaritans complained to Augustus about Archelaus, and Augustus deposed and exiled him. Judea now became a minor Roman province with Caesarea Maritime as its capital. It was governed first by a prefect and later by a procurator from the *equites* or knights. The governor of Syria became Judea's supervisor, if not in law at least in practice. Antipas would rule until 39 C.E. from Tiberias in Galilee while Philip's reign, from Caesarea Philippi, would end in 34 C.E.

Roman rule in Judea was not calm. From the beginning the Romans did not understand Judaism. The initial takeover of Judea prompted Rome to conduct a census, which proved unpopular because many Jews, probably rightfully, saw it as a prelude to higher taxes. Traditional nationalism coupled with religious fervor prompted groups such as the Zealots and the Sicarii (professional dagger-men) to create dissension. Some members of the Pharisees continued to promote the idea of the Messiah, as did other individuals. On the other hand the Sadducees collaborated with the Romans and continued to hold the high priesthood as they had under Herod's rule. To help maintain order the Romans reinstated the Sanhedrin.

With the death of Augustus in 14 C.E., his stepson Tiberius ruled the Roman Empire. Tiberius's advisor and praetorian prefect was Sejanus, who seems to have not favored the Jews. He was perhaps fearful that autonomous Jewish states such as in Parthia might be favored in Judea, resulting in rebellion. Under Sejanus the prefect Pontius Pilate (25–36) governed the province, keeping Caiaphas, the chief priest, in office throughout his tenure. Pilate became involved in a series of missteps, which can be seen as characteristic of Rome's failure to understand the Jews.

The first dealt with the military standards, which bore the emperor's image. Pilate brought them into Jerusalem, which meant they were near the Temple. Many of the Jews believed that this was a graven image so close to the Temple. After days of protests, most of which was nonviolent, he finally gave in lest an insurrection arise. In another misstep, he used money from a Jewish religious fund to help construct an aqueduct. When protests occurred in Jerusalem he had some Roman agents disguised as Jews attack the protesters. Pilate also erected gilded shields in the Fortress Antonia inscribed with his name and the name of Tiberius. Since he was a protégé of Sejanus, who had been executed in 31, he may have done this to ingratiate himself with the emperor. Protests soon followed, probably based on Tiberius's divine parentage (Augustus, his step- and adoptive father, had been declared a god). This would have upset the Jews because of their monotheistic beliefs and the ban on idols. Finally, in Samaria, a would-be nationalist and messiah urged his followers to climb Mount Gerizim to find Moses's sacred vessels, fearing a full-scale insurrection: if found they would have given Samaria claim over Judea; if not, Rome would have been blamed for destroying them. Pilate prevented the action, inflicting casualties. He then arrested and executed many of the ringleaders. It was this incident that may have prompted his removal by Tiberius. During this time Herod Agrippa I, a grandson of Herod the Great, was ascending the political front in Judea. With the death of Philip and Herod Antipas's disgrace and exile, Herod Agrippa was given their territories and made king.

Tiberius was succeeded by Gaius (commonly known as Caligula), which produced further tensions. The people of Jamnia on the coast of Judea were Greek and Jewish. The Greeks erected an altar in honor of the emperor, which the Jews tore down. Enraged, Caligula decided to follow Antiochus IV Epiphanes's policy of erecting statues of the imperial cult in the Temple and synagogues. He ordered Publius Petronius, the governor of Syria, to erect in the Temple a colossal bronze statue of the emperor in the form of Jupiter, who he thought he was. Petronius delayed, arguing he would need two legions to install the statue because it would lead to rebellion. Moving south, he was met at the border by Herod Agrippa I, who had convinced Caligula not go through with the plan if the Jews would allow the Greeks to honor the emperor. Shortly thereafter Caligula was assassinated.

Caligula's uncle, Claudius, became Rome's emperor, and he in turn increased Herod Agrippa's position by turning Judea over to him. His kingdom now included the lands that his grandfather, Herod the Great, had ruled over. Unlike Herod the Great, Herod Agrippa received support from the Jews. It appears that Agrippa intended to make himself and Judea important in eastern Mediterranean policy. He planned to hold a regional conference of client kings, but the Roman governor of Syria decided not to attend. Rome may have wanted to send a message that these client kings were just that, clients of Rome. Herod's death in 44 C.E., after ruling just three years, made Judea once again a Roman province.

The history of Judea after Herod Agrippa was one of instability and violence. The governors who ruled saw an increase in violence and discontent. Massacres, bandits, economic hardships, and famine pushed Judea further into chaos. Internal religious problems between the different Jewish sects and an offshoot of Judaism, Christianity, further destabilized the region. In 66 things had deteriorated so much that the captain of the Temple, Eleazar, son of the former high priest Ananias, declared that sacrifices from foreigners would no longer be allowed. This meant that the sacrifices for the emperor and Rome, paid by Rome, would not be allowed. This was in effect an act of rebellion, which Eleazar knew. The result was the First Jewish Revolt, which destroyed the fabric of society in Judea. In 69 C.E. the future emperor Titus seized the city and the Temple was burned, either deliberately or accidentally. The siege of Jerusalem became the defining point in first-century C.E. Palestine. The wars began in 66 C.E. and culminated in the siege and capture in 70 C.E. by Titus, the new emperor's son.

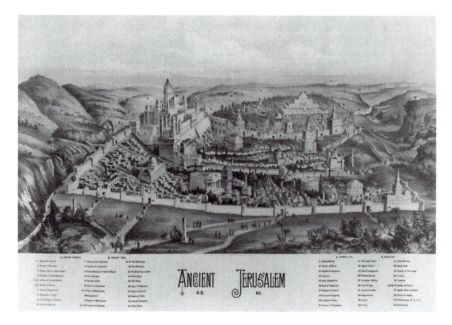

Ancient Jerusalem, 65 C.E. Courtesy of Library of Congress.

In the spring of 69 Vespasian, who had been conducting the war since 66, advanced slowly toward Jerusalem, and when the Jews engaged in civil strife over the conduct of the war, Vespasian decided to avoid attacking Jerusalem and let them squabble. He reduced Samaria, Peraea, and Idumaea instead. In the spring of 69 Vespasian then advanced and began to besiege Jerusalem. When the emperor Nero was overthrown the army elected Vespasian as emperor who then appointed his son Titus as general. Titus now advanced upon the city with a large army. In April Titus began the siege, and he breached the lower city walls in a short time. The Fortress Antonia and the Temple, both heavily fortified, held out. Titus then attempted to starve the Jews out by building an earthen wall around the city. This failed and Titus once again began to besiege the city. On July 5 the Fortress Antonia fell and on August 10 the Temple was taken. The upper city was finally taken on September 7 and Jerusalem was captured. Titus ordered the city to be razed.

The Romans celebrated their victory by building the Arch of Titus, where the Menorah or seven-branched candlestick was engraved. The last pockets of resistance were crushed when Herod the Great's fortress at Masada was seized in 72 by Flavius Silva, although 960 Jewish defenders and their families committed suicide, and only 2 women and 5 children survived. With the rebellion at its end, the Judea of the New Testament ceased to exist.

JOSEPHUS'S ACCOUNT OF THE SIEGE OF JERUSALEM

The following account from Josephus shows the horror of Titus's siege and the conditions in Jerusalem.

4. Now there was a certain woman that dwelt beyond Jordan, her name was Mary; her father was Eleazar, of the village Bethezub, which signifies the *house of Hyssop*. She was eminent for her family and her wealth, and had fled away to Jerusalem with the rest of the multitude, and was with them besieged therein at this time. The other effects of this woman had been already seized upon, such I mean as she had brought with her out of Perea, and removed to the city. What she had treasured up besides, as also what food she had contrived to save, had also been carried off by the rapacious guards, who came every day running into her house for that purpose. This put the poor woman into a very great passion, and by the frequent reproaches and imprecations she cast at these rapacious villains, she had provoked them to anger against her; but none of them, either out of the indignation she had raised against herself, or out of commiseration of her case, would take away her life; and if she found any food, she perceived her labours were for others, and not for herself; and it was now become impossible for her any way to find any more food, while the famine pierced through her very bowels and marrow, when also her passion was fired to a degree beyond the famine itself, nor did she consult with any thing but with her passion and the necessity she was in. She then attempted a most unnatural thing; and snatching up her son, who was

a child sucking at her breast, she said, "O thou miserable infant! for whom shall I preserve thee in this war, this famine, and this sedition? As to the war with the Romans, if they preserve our lives, we must be slaves. This famine also will destroy us, even before that slavery comes upon us; yet are these seditious rogues more terrible than both the other. Come on; be thou my food, and be thou a fury to these seditious varlets, and a bye-word to the world, which is all that is now wanting to complete the calamities of us Jews." As soon as she had said this, she slew her son; and then roasted him, and ate the one half of him, and kept the other half by her concealed. Upon this the seditious came in presently, and smelling the horrid scent of this food, they threatened her, that they would cut her throat immediately, if she did not show them what food she had gotten ready. She replied, that she had saved a very fine portion of it for them; and withal uncovered what was left of her son. Hereupon they were seized with a horror and amazement of mind, and stood astonished at the sight; when she said to them, "This is mine own son; and what hath been done was mine own doing! Come, eat of this food; for I have eaten of it myself! Do not you pretend to be either more tender than a woman, or more compassionate than a mother; but if you be so scrupulous, and do abominate this my sacrifice, as I have eaten the one half, let the rest be reserved for me also." After which, those men went out trembling, being never so much affrighted at any thing as they were at this, and with some difficulty they left the rest of that meat to the mother. Upon which the whole city was full of horrid action immediately; and while every body laid this miserable case before their own eyes, they trembled, as if this unheard-of action had been done by themselves. So those that were thus distressed by the famine were very desirous to die, and those already dead were esteemed happy, because they had not lived long enough either to hear or to see such miseries.

Source: The Works of Josephus, trans., William Whiston (William Milner Cheapside, 1850), Book 6.3.4, *War of the Jews,* pp. 602–3.

PAUL IN THE GREEK EAST

The New Testament, however, is not just the story of Palestine. After the Gospels, the New Testament continues with the Acts of the Apostles. In this work the spread of Christianity is presented. The main character in this book is Paul. The travels of Paul were throughout the eastern Mediterranean, through Asia Minor, Greece, and Cyprus. Ultimately the book of Acts ends with Paul's voyage to Rome, capital of the Roman Empire.

The regions of Paul's travels were Greek, not Jewish. The letters of Paul and other early Christian writers were mainly written to the Greek converts to Christianity. This culture was quite different than that of Palestine. Unlike a region controlled by the monotheistic religion of Judaism, the Greek regions were originally pagan. The political history was also different. While both cultures were controlled by kings, the Greek east revered its leaders and in some cases viewed them as gods. In addition, the Greek east, combined with the ancient Persian rule, further made the local population to view its leaders as gods or superhuman. As the Romans moved in and controlled the region, the eastern Mediterranean now became absorbed by the Roman state.

Originally a republic, the Romans ultimately adopted many of the Greek and Near Eastern customs of leadership. Although Augustus was careful not to declare himself a god in the west, there is evidence that in the east he allowed the Greek culture to prevail and to hail him as a god. The Roman state allowed the local communities to rule themselves as before. This meant that Rome merely controlled the top while the local communities elected their own rulers. For Rome these communities continued to be Greek and not Roman. The local communities were a conglomeration of various groups. There would have been some Romans, especially in the larger communities. Made up of soldiers and ex-soldiers, the Romans composed the top of societies. Many of them were colonists established by Augustus after his victory to ensure control. Below these upper echelons were the local leaders. These were the successors of previous elites who had held power for generations. Under the Romans they controlled the local government, which gave them power and prestige. Beneath this group would have been the middle class. Often made up of new groups from the local communities, the middle class often made its ascent through economic opportunities that the Roman peace allowed. Ultimately at the bottom were the peasants, those whose ancestors had been peasants and whose descendents would continue to be so. In addition to the local population were other individuals who would have been in the communities. Foreigners would have included Jews who had begun to emigrate out of Palestine.

These Jews who made up the Diaspora were not exiles, but rather individuals who had emigrated to convert and establish separate communities outside of Palestine. The Jews would have set up their own synagogues, which now became the center of their local religion. This institution would have been the center for the Jewish faith. The synagogue allowed the Jews to maintain their identity inside this pagan and Greek community. The local population was then divided into separate groups, which were clearly defined. When Paul arrived in these communities he would have found Jewish groups that had lived in these areas for generations.

Within this historical framework there was a division between the rural villages and the cities. The rural villages tended to be more conservative, clinging to the traditional and previous ways. The cities were more open to new ideas because the population tended to interact with various groups. This interaction allowed the flow of information and ideas to mix. The cities were more likely to be influenced by Hellenistic and Roman ideas than the rural villages. Herod the Great built a new Hellenistic city, Caesarea, on the Mediterranean shore. This city became the link between Palestine and the rest of the Roman world. Unlike Jerusalem, which remained Jewish because of its ancient religious connection, Caesarea was Greek. Herod preferred to reside in cities like Caesarea, as opposed to Jerusalem. When Rome took over, the governor made this Hellenistic city its capital because it had the amenities an upper-class Roman would expect. The city had a bath, hippodrome, theater, and other Greek structures.

BIOGRAPHIES OF JOHN OF GISCHALA, TITUS, AND JOSEPHUS

John of Gischala

John of Gischala, one of the leaders in the Jewish war, was a personal enemy of Josephus. Both men commanded armies in the north in Galilee at the beginning of the rebellion. After this region had been conquered he fled south with his troops. He arrived in Jerusalem where he soon became prominent, so much that he appointed a high priest, Phannias. Josephus claims that John behaved like a tyrant. His actions prompted a power struggle between his followers and Eleazar ben Simon, who led the Zealots. John controlled the New or Lower Town of Jerusalem while Eleazar occupied the Temple. A third party, Simon bar Giora, controlled the Old or Upper Town and viewed himself as leader of a messianic movement. During the Passover of 70 C.E. Eleazar allowed individuals to enter the Temple to perform the sacrifices; John and his men used the sword to seize the area, forcing Eleazar's men to surrender.

The struggle between the three men weakened the fighting forces in Jerusalem. John wanted to strike against the Roman legions but feared that Simon would not let him back in the city, leaving him to be captured. John therefore did not attack, which allowed the Romans to continue building a surrounding wall. John and Simon's men joined together after the Romans breached the outer walls. After five days the second wall was breached and the Romans entered the city. John's men were able to thwart the new attacks and Titus realized that the siege would take even more time and energy, costing more Roman lives. Titus now changed his tactics and planned to starve the Jews out of Jerusalem. Titus ordered his men to continue their assault on the Fortress Antonia and to enter the tunnel that John's men had dug. The Romans captured the fortress and after a hard struggle forced John and his men out of the Temple. Ultimately the Fortress Antonia was demolished and the Temple was taken. The Temple was burned either by the order of Titus (more probably) or by accident (Josephus's story). After entering the city John and his men fled into the sewers, where after a few days he surrendered.

John appears not to have viewed himself as the Messiah. When Titus captured Jerusalem John was brought before him. Titus took him back to Rome where he imprisoned John for the rest of his life. Simon was likewise taken to Rome where he was executed.

Titus

Titus, born in 39 C.E., was emperor from 79 until his death in 81 and was best known for his campaigns and capture of Jerusalem. He was brought up in the court of Claudius and was a friend of the emperor's son Brittanicus. His military career began in Germany in 57, and he served in Britain in 60 during the rebellion of Boudicca. Upon his return to Rome he married Arrecina Tertulla, in 63 having a daughter Julia Flavia; his wife died in 65 and he married Marcia Furnilla, whom he divorced due to her family's connection with a conspiracy against the emperor Nero. Titus did not remarry. Titus was stationed in Egypt when the Jewish rebellion broke out. He took the 15th Legion out of Egypt and joined his father in Judea.

After the war Titus celebrated victory games in Caesarea and Beirut. He received a crown from the Parthian king Vologases I, probably as a sign of submission on the part of the Parthians. He returned to Rome and celebrated a triumph in which he had the Great Menorah carried through the streets. In the triumphal procession was Simon Bar Giora, who was then executed in the Roman Forum. During this time the sister of King Agrippa II, Queen Berenice of Cilicia, lived openly with him in the palace. Denounced by Cynics who feared an oriental queen, Titus sent her away.

His career under his father was not the most sterling. As commander of the guard he was forced to ensure the safety of his father. This often included acting violently against his enemies. With his elevation to the emperorship many feared that Titus would be another Nero with his vices. Instead he attempted and succeeded in becoming well-liked by the populace. He eliminated the treason trials, did not persecute the senate, eliminated the informants by banishing them, and when Berenice attempted to return to his favor he had her sent away.

During his reign there were two major disasters, a fire in Rome and the eruption of Vesuvius, which buried Pompeii. He completed the Coliseum and constructed his baths over Nero's private palace, the Golden House, On September 13, 81, he contracted a fever and died.

Josephus

Josephus, son of Matthias, was born in 37 and fought in the Jewish rebellion of 66–70 C.E. In 67 he became a prisoner and ingratiated himself with Vespasian by declaring that he would be made emperor. When this turned out to come true his stature increased. Vespasian is best known for two works, *Jewish Antiquities* and the *War of the Jews*. Viewed by many Jews as a traitor and collaborator, Josephus appears to have written his work with two purposes involved, to refute this charge and to exonerate Vespasian and Titus. He attempted to explain Judaism to the Romans and in many ways wanted to attempt reconciliation between the Jews and Romans.

Josephus was granted Roman citizenship by Vespasian. His family life was not idyllic. His first wife and his parents died in Jerusalem during the rebellion. During the war Vespasian presented him a Jewish woman captured by the Romans. This woman left him around the time of the siege of

Jerusalem. He then married another Jewish woman from Alexandria with whom he had three children. Divorcing his third wife, Josephus around 75 married a Jewish woman from Crete. He had two sons by her. It is difficult to know the complete story of his personal life; what is clear is that within a short time, seven years, he had four wives.

As a military leader Josephus was not successful. As a family man he did not have long and successful marriages. But as a historian, Josephus was able to ensure his reputation and, more importantly, relate the history of the period of the New Testament.

2

DAILY LIFE OF GEOGRAPHICAL GROUPS IN PALESTINE

Joseph also went up from Galilee, out of the city of Nazareth, into Judea, to the city of David, which is called Bethlehem, because he was of the house and lineage of David. (Luke 2:4)

For the Romans Palestine was a single province separating Egypt and Syria, Rome's two most important regions in the east. Syria protected the valuable heartland of Asia Minor and the path into Egypt, the grain land of empire. Palestine, the traditional route along the coastline, connected the two. Although Palestine's land was not especially rich, its position was.

GALILEE

Palestine was home to numerous groups, as witnessed in the New Testament. There were of course Jews, but this group can be further divided into territorial groupings. In the north was Galilee, which had received Judaism, at times forcibly, around 100 B.C.E. The area was small, 50 miles long and 25 wide. What was most pronounced in the region was the Sea or Lake of Galilee, 13 by 8 miles, located on the eastern side of the region. Interestingly the area was the most populous of Jewish lands; Josephus stated that during the great rebellion three million people lived in the region with about 240 towns engaged in ship building, harvesting timber, fishing, and trading circling the Sea of Galilee. In addition, roads ran throughout Galilee, as opposed to Judea, connecting the region to elements outside Palestine.

These roads connected Galilee with the Mediterranean, which allowed merchants to bring in goods from throughout the Roman Empire, while the coastline had pottery and cloth-dying factories. A Jewish proverb said if you wish to get rich, go to Galilee. In addition to the economic wealth of Galilee, the region was noted for its nationalism, becoming the center for insurrection. Not noted for their observance of Jewish law, especially dietary rules, another popular saying was that no prophet comes from Galilee. These views are consistently seen in the New Testament. The hills and mountains provided refuge for the brigands and rebels who constantly operated there. It would ultimately take a man raised and trained in the hills to defeat the indigenous rebels, and that man was Herod the Great. The future king in his mid-twenties destroyed the leaders of the insurrection with such brutality that not only was there no more problem (which pleased Rome), but the Jewish Sanhedrin in Judea censured him.

Galilee became an economic center with small trade and industry. The New Testament relates that Jesus' father Joseph was a carpenter, a skilled craftsman, which would have made him a respected member of the middle class (Matt. 13:55). Jesus' followers Peter, John, Andrew, and James were fishermen on the Sea of Galilee who appeared to have owned their own boats, suggesting that they were more than just laborers (Matt. 4:18–20). Jesus' parables often relate occupations such as potters, farmers, vine dressers, and merchants. Jesus must have been familiar with these occupations and they must have been common enough for his audience to know about them to form a picture in their minds when the stories were related. Galilee should therefore be seen as having a varied work force, which diversified the economy of the region.

Ethnically the Galileans were similar to the inhabitants of Judea, but historically they were polytheists. The Assyrians under Tiglath-Pileser III (730s B.C.E.) conquered the region and imported a large mixed population into the area. After Alexander the Great's conquest (333 B.C.E.) the region became more Hellenized than the south. The Pharisees did not consider the Galileans' conversion valid because it was forced upon them during the rule of John Hyrcanus I. The inhabitants at the time of Jesus were therefore a mixture of Jews and pagans, probably in equal portions. This may in part explain the hostility between their leaders and Jesus. Although probably similar in most ways to Judeans, Galileans were seen as outsiders and looked down upon, as backwards theologians and violators of the dietary laws. They could not trace their heritage back to the Temple of Solomon. But Galilee was crucial to the daily life mentioned in the New Testament because this was Jesus' residence.

While it is doubtful that Jesus was born in Bethlehem in Judea, more probably in or near Nazareth, the Gospels clearly indicate that Jesus spent most of his life in the northern region. In the Gospels Jesus spent most of his time preaching in Galilee, and it was only in the final months that he took his message into Judea. But his preaching in Galilee was confined to the smaller towns. For example Jesus avoided Herod Antipas's capital Tiberias; he may have wished to avoid Herod and his court, especially after John the Baptist had been executed by Herod. The chief towns mentioned in the Gospels were Nazareth, Cana, Capernaum, and Tiberias, mentioned as Herod's capital. Galilee lay on the crossroads of both the east and west. The roads that passed through Galilee connected the region not only geographically with both regions but culturally. To the east lay the oriental kingdom of Parthia, which had connections to the ancient Persian, Babylonian, Assyrian, and Greek cultures. To the west lay Greece and Rome with its traditions. Galilee in between received both cultures while receiving its major religious, ethnic, and historical influence from the south, Jewish Judea.

One of the chief cities was Damascus, in the interior, which linked both regions via the ancient caravan routes. These routes brought Palestine into contact with the nomadic tribes of the Arabian Desert. This contact further added to the cultural interaction that happened in this region. The mix of cultures would shape not only the first century B.C.E. and C.E. periods culturally, but economically, politically, and religiously. For example, from the east came the ideas of dualism seen in ancient Persian religion. This dualism postulated the struggle between good and evil. From the east, Greece, and the west, Egypt, came the Hellenistic religious view of rebirth. From Greece, the rebirth of Dionysius and Demeter, and from Egypt, the Hellenized god Osiris, both influenced the belief in the resurrection of the body. With the nomadic lifestyle and caravans crossing from the deserts these different ideas came into contact and allowed for the mixing of beliefs.

TRANSJORDANIAN REGION

To the east of Galilee lay Herod Antipas's brother Philip's kingdom. Philip was the son of Herod the Great and Cleopatra of Jerusalem and the husband of Salome, Herodias's daughter. He was tetrarch of the Transjordanian region of Ituraea, Batanaea, Trachonitis, Araunitis, Gaulanities, and Panias. Philip built the city of Caesarea Philippi. Philip's region likewise held a large number of pagans, perhaps the majority. The region held a large number of Greek or Hellenized inhabitants. This region had a heavy Greek influence due to the colonies established after Alexander the Great's conquest. This region was probably more Hellenized than the other regions. Occupations in this region would have been similar to Galilee, but with perhaps a bit more mercantile influence due to the Greek towns. These inhabitants were descendents from Macedonian settlers who established cities along the lines of Greek cities. This region, which had not been heavily influenced by the Jews, was in many ways a refuge for dissidents escaping Herod Antipas's rule. Philip constantly looked for ways to embarrass his brother by not only providing safe haven, but also supporting religious elements who challenged Herod.

After John the Baptist's execution, Jesus left Galilee and traveled by boat to Bethsaida where he continued to preach (Mark 6:45). As in Galilee, Jesus avoided the larger towns of Philip's territory because they were predominately pagan. What is clear from Jesus' preaching in Galilee and in Philip's region was that he tended to reach out to the rural or at least powerful small town inhabitants in predominately Jewish towns and avoided the large cosmopolitan pagan towns. Jesus also intentionally avoided large towns due to potential problems with the authorities, who may have attempted to forcibly detain him. Without many followers, and with those he had mainly attracted from the rural regions, Jesus, and John before him, would have been hard pressed to remain free. Avoiding these areas was in their best interest. The political infighting between the successors of Herod the Great ensured some protection for various dissident groups from either side. The difference between the two regions also extended to their views on religion. Herod Antipas, ruling in a predominately Jewish land, had to always be careful of upsetting the local population with his ideas of ruling like his father, an oriental despot. He could not behave like a Greek ruler, while his brother had some leeway because most of his region was pagan and heavily influenced by the Greeks. In both regions the concept of the Roman-Greek economy prevailed. Relying on mercantile exchange, the region imported and exported goods to and from all regions of the Eastern Mediterranean. These goods, many of which were luxury items, found their way throughout society.

SAMARIA

South of Galilee lay Samaria. A country known for its wild boars, stags, and other animals, it provided a link between Galilee and Judea. Here, the inhabitants were closely related to the Jews of Judea but claimed an alternate interpretation of Moses and the Torah. The disagreements between the Jews of Judea and Samaria were religious and political. When the Assyrians under Sargon II conquered Samaria in 722 b.c.e. and Nebuchadnezzar of Babylon seized Jerusalem in 587 b.c.e, both regions suffered deportations. The inhabitants of both areas developed their own religious, political, and economic power. Later Jews would claim that Samaria was inhabited by foreigners, but most of the inhabitants were the descendents from earlier occupants of the old Northern Kingdom of Israel. These inhabitants clung to their religious and political ideas of the Northern Kingdom, especially in that they held too many of the pre-prophetic ideas that argued for local territorial religious ideas. Hence the idea that Mt. Gerizim was more important than Jerusalem. The situation changed when the new power Persia under Cyrus allowed the Jews in Babylon to return to Judea. The Samaritans probably feared the revival of the Jewish state in the south and made overtures to Jerusalem to prevent the Jerusalem wall from being rebuilt. The Samaritans feared that a strong Judea might cause the Persians to rethink their policy and force the region to submit.

After Alexander's conquest the Samaritans renounced Jerusalem's religious influence, declaring that they were the true descendents of Moses's law, that their ancient holy site at Mt. Gerizim was the true center of Judaism and not the recent city of Jerusalem (only the center since David), and that the Pentateuch, written in Hebrew and not Aramaic (the language adopted by the Babylonian refugees) was authoritative. The Samaritan religion, which placed its emphasis on the Pentateuch and the book of Joshua, can be seen as a conservative sect within Judaism. Nevertheless, because they never reasserted their political independence and authority, and because they were often surrounded by more powerful states, both Jewish and pagan, the Samaritans received influences from both Jews and gentiles. When the Jewish state was not so powerful the Samaritans disclaimed their Jewish heritage and sought to align themselves more with the Sidonians due to their descent from Canaanite-Phoenician stock. Because the Samaritans collaborated with Antiochus Epiphanes and temporarily dedicated their temple at Gerizim to the Greek god Zeus, the Jews viewed them as traitors, gentiles, or heretics.

When the Jewish state revived its fortune after Antiochus, Samaria was now directly influenced from the south. Ultimately John Hyrcanus destroyed the Samaritan rival temple on Mt. Gerizim. In the New Testament period the Jews viewed the Samaritans almost as gentiles. Herod the Great ruled over Samaria with some success because he likewise was not completely Jewish. Because Herod came from a region that was recently converted, and at times forcibly, he had a greater affinity for Samaria than had his Jewish predecessors. Many in Samaria viewed him without disdain, unlike the Jews.

Herod the Great would build a palace in the city of Samaria, now renamed Sebaste (the Greek name for Augustus), which was more Greek than Samaritan. The city had been rebuilt by Pompey, and Herod made it even more impressive with towers and walls. After Herod's death his son Archelaus brutalized the Samaritans, while under the Romans the Samaritans were often at odds with the central government. Pontius Pilate massacred Samaritans who attempted to seize Mt. Gerizim; their protest to the governor of Syria resulted in his recall to Rome.

The writers and readers of the New Testament mainly viewed the inhabitants of Samaria with disdain. Although probably ethnically similar to the inhabitants of Judea, they were clearly seen as inferior and non-Jewish (Luke 9:51). Jesus restricted his disciples from going into Samaria on religious grounds. His enemies would call him a Samaritan, a derogatory remark (John 8:48). The Samaritans for their part were not above causing discomfort to the Jewish authorities, especially concerning the sacrifices in the Jerusalem Temple or with the liturgical calendar emanating from Jerusalem. For example, once they attempted to defile the sanctuary by throwing bones in the Temple, and another time they lit beacons (a common practice in antiquity to send a message) misleadingly to announce to the Diaspora the beginning of a new month according to a calendar at times different than that determined by the authorities in Jerusalem. In one of their texts the story was told of how two Samaritan youths replaced the doves destined for sacrifice in the temple by a Jewish pilgrim with mice, which were not discovered until after his arrival in Jerusalem and set into motion (although unspecified in the story as to how) the destruction of the Temple. While not all of the writers of the New Testament were Jewish, the general bias against the Samaritans remained. This bias was probably due to the original followers of Jesus, as well as Paul, who had natural antipathy toward the Samarians. This region acted as a buffer between the northern Syrian Greeks and the southern Judean Jews after the establishment of the independent Jewish state in the second century B.C.E. This buffer situation, however, allowed the Jews to receive the influx of Greek ideas without coming into direct contact with the purely pagan lands. Although viewed with disdain, the Samaritans nevertheless provided important cultural and economic connections.

The region of Samaria had occupations similar to the other regions. Agriculture must have made up most of the livelihood and workforce. A component of agriculture seen in all of the regions would have been sheep-herding. Sheep, and to a lesser extent goats, were important commodities in the region, providing food and clothing for the inhabitants. South of Samaria lay the traditional heartland of Judaism, the region of Judea.

JUDEA

The Jews of Judea claimed descent from the kingdom of David. This is only partially true, for even here the inhabitants were not homogeneous. During David's time there were mercenaries who became part of society, for example Uriah the Hittite. During the time of Solomon and his successors there was a continual absorption of new ethnic members into society. And after the fall of Jerusalem in 587 some of the population, the majority of the political and social elites, was taken to Babylon where they endured over 50 years of captivity before they returned. It is probable that some individuals married into the local community. When the descendents returned they would have brought back some of the new converts and family members. These individuals would then intermingle with the remnants of those who had not been taken to Babylon. These remnants again probably received an influx of new members from outside of Judea, namely Babylonians, but also Egyptians, Assyrians, and Phoenicians.

The region of Judea was probably more settled than Samaria or Idumaea. Although agriculture still remained the dominant economic force, mercantile opportunities continuously existed. One such opportunity that was explicitly Jewish was the business of the Temple. The Temple, more than just a religious site, was the philosophical and religious center of Judaism. Here the celebration of the religion provided interaction for all Jews and even gentiles. Economically all Jews were to provide payment of taxes to the Temple, the so called Temple tax. This tax provided upkeep for the Temple. In addition gentiles, in particular the Roman emperor, provided funds so that sacrifices could be offered in the name of the Roman emperor for the safety of the emperor. This was not offering sacrifices to the emperor but rather for his safety. Furthermore, individuals who wished to offer sacrifices, for example doves, had to pay for the victims in Temple coin, meaning that Roman or city coinage had to be exchanged for Temple coin. This simple transaction provided numerous occupations: animal providers, butchers, money changers, and priests. The Temple economy was of major importance to the city of Jerusalem.

JERUSALEM

Being the largest and most important city in Palestine, Jerusalem had a commanding importance in the economy and society of Judea. The city acted as the political center for Judaism. Herod the Great constructed a fortress next to the Temple, the Antonia, named after Marc Antony, which not only protected the city, but allowed Herod to "watch" over the Temple. It was in the Antonia that Pontius Pilate the governor questioned and judged Jesus. Herod also constructed a palace nearby that was used as his seat of power. In the New Testament this palace was occupied by Herod Antipas and was the scene of his interview with Jesus after Pilate had transferred jurisdiction. The city also was the economic center of Judea. Here merchants negotiated with each other for goods traveling in and out of the region. Goods from all over the Roman Empire were traded and provided important contact with individuals outside of Judea. Finally the city was the social center for the entire region. The elites, especially the Sadducees who controlled the Temple, were able to exert influence over all Judaism. The city remained the seat of power for Judaism until the defeat of Bar Kochba during the reign of Hadrian. Judea was the most important district in the east for Rome. Although Rome viewed the Jews as quarrelsome, the district was crucial for controlling the routes between the eastern province of Syria and western Egypt. These two regions were crucial to Roman military and economic survival. Into this was mixed the Jewish religion. Since the Romans needed the region they had to constantly interact with the Jews. This interaction unfortunately led to constant conflict. These conflicts evoked strong passions because there was no middle ground.

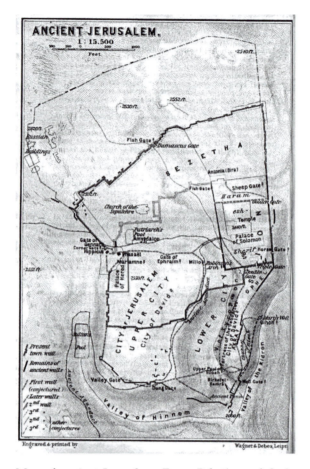

Map of ancient Jerusalem. From *Palestine and Syria: Handbook for Travellers* by Karl Baedeker, 5th ed., 1912. University of Texas Libraries.

EDOM

To the south of Judea, another region of more recent conversion was Idumea, Greek for Edom, where Herod the Great's family had come from. The territory was from the Dead Sea southeast to the Gulf of Aqaba. Devoid of occupation until the thirteenth century B.C.E., the region was occupied by a Semitic tribe ethnically related to the Hebrews. David conquered the region, and after Alexander's conquest it was taken over by the Arab Nabataeans, who established the Arab kingdom of Idumea from Moab to the gulf with Petra as its capital. The Edomites rejoiced in the destruction of Jerusalem in 587 B.C.E., and many prophets spoke concerning the hostility of Edom and Judea. The region had been attacked by Judea after the Maccabean wars. Judea not only subjected the people politically but also religiously, forcing them to accept Judaism or face exile. This was the first time that a group had been forced into conversion by the Jews. The Idumeans acknowledged Esau, son of Isaac, as their progenitor. But the Idumeans remained pagan, and when Judaism was forced upon them many if not most paid only lip service to Judaism. Their humiliation soon reversed with the accession of Herod, who was a son of an Idumean (recent Jew) and an Arabian (pagan) princess. His ancestry and most likely his outlook made him more pagan (and cosmopolitan) than Jewish. This region, however, was sufficiently Jewish to send a large contingent of troops to Jerusalem, about 20,000, in the great Jewish rebellion of 66 C.E. Vespasian marched into the region and took two towns, Betobris and Caphartoba, killing, according to Josephus, 10 thousand inhabitants. It was also in this region that the great fortress of Masada was occupied by the rebels until destroyed in 73 C.E. by general Silva; two centuries earlier the region had been completely pagan and now it was the last stronghold of the Jewish rebellion. In terms of daily life during the New Testament times, Idumea should be seen as a Jewish region.

The region of Idumea was considered nomadic, with most of the inhabitants engaged in pastoral life. Many of the inhabitants, especially before their conquest by Judea, were nomads who traveled across the deserts into Arabia and Egypt. This land was harsh and few settled sites existed. In many ways the land and its people looked more to the south and west away from Judea than toward the Mediterranean and the Jewish state. The Nabataeans controlled the caravan routes that linked the Persian Gulf, Arabia, and Egypt with Syria. They controlled the city of Damascus after 37 C.E., when Paul was converted and had to escape the city by being lowered from the walls in a hamper. The region, however, did provide some contact with other non-Roman/Greek civilizations. Coming into the region were goods, mainly spices, arrived from India and Arabia. These luxury items did result in the flow of gold coins from the Roman Empire. The Roman writer Pliny the Elder remarked that the flow of gold from the empire to the east was a drain on the economy. This view, however, is not exactly accurate, because the Romans received luxury items. However, this trade did not benefit the average resident, as the goods were destined for Rome.

PHOENICIA AND SYRIA

The coastal region of Palestine held the great Phoenician cities of Tyre, Sidon, and Byblos. These cities, ethnically Semitic, had traditionally looked to the sea and the commerce it brought rather than inland. The New Testament indicates that Jesus had some contact with the coastal cities, and during the early missionary activities his followers also visited them. These cities were cosmopolitan, because after Alexander the Great there was an influx of Greeks. This influx, here and among other cities, brought with it Hellenism. The region allowed for the exchange of goods and ideas throughout the Mediterranean. Greek ideas affected not only with the local pagan populations but the Jewish residents, which allowed for the creation of new cultural, religious, and social concepts.

Further north lay Syria. Syria consists of a series of north-south fertile belts parallel to the coast. The northern coastal plain is narrow, confined by the sea and the Lebanon Mountains. In Palestine the plain broadens into the Judean and Samarian plateaus and contained strategic ports at Gaza, Antioch, Tyre, and Sidon. Antioch was the most important city. Antioch commanded the route to the Euphrates and to Asia Minor either by the Gulf of Alexandretta or across the Amanus range via the Vailan Pass. The Syrians were a conglomeration of different ethnic groups. This region had seen in the past millennium the Hittites, Assyrians, Babylonians, Persians, Greeks, and Romans, although most were probably Assyrians. This region, pagan, had traditionally been the jumping-off point for an invasion of Palestine. During the New Testament Syria was the major Roman province, which protected not only Palestine but Asia Minor from the Parthians and Persians. The chief city was Antioch, a Greek city, which Peter and Paul visited, converting many. From Antioch Paul traveled to Asia Minor and Greece. These regions contained some Jewish communities but the majority of the population was Greek.

The Greeks in these regions were descendents not only of Alexander's followers, but of much earlier arrivals. During the eighth century B.C.E. a great migration and colonization movement from Greece occurred. Settling mainly on the coastline, these colonists established cities that would rival many cities in Greece itself: Ephesus, Melitus, and Rhodes. In addition to the Greeks, Asia Minor had witnessed an invasion from the north by the Gauls in the third century B.C.E. Their descendents, who had settled in the northern region, were the Galatians, to whom Paul wrote his letter.

ASIA MINOR AND ITS HISTORY

Asia Minor was a group of ancient lands that had existed for nearly a millennium. After the arrival of nomadic groups around 1000 B.C.E, the fabric of the ancient eastern Mediterranean population was destroyed. A group known as the Sea Peoples, a misnomer in an ancient Egyptian text, had devastated Palestine and the east. A group that was destroyed in Asia Minor was the kingdom of the Hittites. After their destruction a series of kingdoms arose in Asia Minor, the Lydians, Lycians, and Carians. After the dark ages in Greece following the fall of Mycenaean power to the rise of the ancient Greek city states around 700 B.C.E, Greek colonists arrived on the western shore of Asia Minor. Most of the cities on the coast were now Greek. In the New Testament the Epistle to the Ephesians is written to the descendents of these Greek colonists.

Around the year 270 B.C.E. another group arrived in Asia Minor, the Gauls, who moved across from Europe. The Gauls ultimately carved out their own kingdom, and again we find a letter to their descendents in

Paul's letter to the Galatians. Under the early empire Galatia was east of Bithynia and included the ancient Paphlagonia, northeastern Phrygia, and a part of western Cappadocia. The southern part, lying on both sides of the river Halys, was Galatia proper.

Asia Minor was a land composed of several distinct geographical regions. Along the coast near Syria was Cilicia. For the Romans, the acquisition of Cilicia ended the major threat of the pirates during the end of the republic, but unfortunately, the area produced brigands, attested throughout the time of Rome's control. The early province of Cilicia lay east of Pamphylia and south of Cappadocia, reaching the south coast of Asia Minor form Coracesium to Alexandria. The eastern portion of the province was known as Campestris and the western as Montana or Aspers. For the most part the coastal regions, at 300 to 1,500 feet, rise rapidly to over 6,000 feet in the mountains. At Seleucia the coastal road, running west to Anemurium and Selinus, split into the mountain road to Claudiopolis, and then to Laranda, where it ran into the east-west road to Derbe and Tyana. The coastal road continued from Issus west to Adana and Tarsus. At Tarsus the road split, one west and other north through the Cilician Gates to Podandus, Faustinopolis, and Tyana. These regions would have been known by Paul, as witnessed by his Letters to the Galatians, Colossians, and seen in his travels in the Acts of Apostles to Pamphylia and Pisidia (13.4–14.28).

In the north lay the Pontus region, with mountains over 3,000 feet high, which is modern-day northern Turkey on the southern coast of the Black Sea. The original province of Cappadocia adjoined Galatia and Pamphylia toward the east. It too had four regions: Lycaonia, the most western next to Isauria and Asia; Cappadocia proper, east of Lycaonia on both sides of the river Haylys; Pontus, north of Cappadocia proper, to the Euxine or Black Sea; and Armenia Minor, southeast of Pontus, lying along the upper Euphrates. This entire region was rough, and with the mountains dividing and separating the regions, individual cities were often cut off from communities only a few miles away. These cities had numerous distinct communities.

Paul also visited the ancient land of Greece. In a series of letters we see not only the message Paul imparted, but the trouble he had with the new converts. His letter to the Thessalonians refers to the city of Thessalonica. His letter to the Philippians refers to the city of Philippi, the ancient city established by Philip of Macedon, Alexander the Great's father. Finally there was the letter to the Corinthians, referring to the city of Corinth.

In the New Testament, especially the letters of Paul indicate that Jews were not the only groups who received Jesus' message. The different ethnic groups existed in a much wider environment, the Roman world. Although the number of Romans from Italy was not great, they were nevertheless present (Matt. 8:5). The Italians were the favored class. They had been settled in this region after the great civil wars, especially after Augustus had demobilized the army. These individuals provided the region with Western ideas and contacts with Italy.

The New Testament makes reference to the West. Paul's letters to the Romans indicate an early Christian community in Rome, which may have been composed not only of Jews but gentiles. Later this community split from the Jewish population, probably during the reign of Claudius, and became composed mainly of gentiles. The letters of Paul to the different communities show the differences between the Jewish world and the gentile.

The Greek world presents us with a different society and lands. The New Testament mentions numerous Greek areas. The first areas visited outside of Palestine were Syria, Cyprus, and Asia Minor.

The regions and peoples mentioned in the New Testament show the great variety of life during the first century c.e. That an individual, such as Paul, could travel from one region to the next meeting a variety of individuals clearly indicates the vitality and complexity of Palestine. Without the national restrictions of modern travel, individuals in a short journey could encounter Roman, Greeks, Jews, Syrians, Egyptians, Babylonians, Persians, and even Ethiopians of a variety of pagan and Jewish sects. All of these factors made the daily life portrayed in the New Testament complex.

3

Nonreligious Influences: Language, Art, and Hellenistic Culture

...began to speak with other tongues as the Spirit gave them utterance...And how hear we every man in our own tongue, wherein we were born? Parthians, and Medes, and Elamites, and the dwellers in Mesopotamia, and in Judaea, and Cappadocia, in Pontus, and Asia, Phrygia, and Pamphylia, in Egypt, and in the parts of Libya about Cyrene, and strangers of Rome, Jews and proselytes, Cretes and Arabians we do hear them speak in our tongues...(Acts 2:4, 8–11)

LANGUAGE

When one picks up the Bible and reads it, they do so in their native tongue or the vernacular. Many Christians forget that the original language of the Old Testament is Hebrew and that the New Testament was transmitted in Greek. When reading the Gospels, Acts, and letters of Paul in English, Spanish, or German one forgets that these are merely translations in which the original meaning is often lost or subtly changed. For example, the Latin word *pax* is often translated as peace. For modern readers it is often taken to mean the absence of war through contention. But for the Romans *pax* meant the complete and utter destruction of the enemy; for it is only by destroying one's enemy that peace could be achieved. This misconception, or even mistranslation, allows for the change in language and its meaning.

Language is a powerful force and it shapes how society views others and oneself. Immigrants to a new country often find it advantageous to learn the language of the host country in order to succeed, while native inhabitants often are fearful of immigrants who speak a strange tongue. But even the Bible in its original language as transmitted today is not necessarily the language of the founders. Jesus most likely did not speak Hebrew or Greek, but rather Aramaic. Furthermore, he spoke a distinct dialect of Aramaic, one of several in Palestine. To fully comprehend the daily lives of those living during the time of the New Testament, it is important to understand all of the language variants and how they impacted society.

The catalog of places mentioned previously in Acts, with the probable later inclusion of Judea, presented the regional languages of the Jewish Diaspora from the east to the west. Most of the languages are of Aramaic stock and many were not distinct languages but rather dialects of Aramaic. The language of Jesus was different from that of High Priest Caiaphas in Jerusalem, even though both spoke Aramaic. The authorities declared that Jesus was a Galilean, and that charge was in part made because of his speech.

Ancient Semitic Languages

The languages of Palestine were complicated. The Old Testament Jews spoke Hebrew, which was a Semitic language. The Semitic languages are a large family that includes Akkadian, Canaanite, Aramaic, Arabic, Ethiopian, and others. The Canaanite language had subgroups that included Phoenician and Hebraic. Hebraic was further subdivided into Moabite, Hebrew, Edomite, and Ammonite. Syrian, another subgroup of Canaanite languages, included Aramaic.[1] Aramaic became the dominant language in the Near East after the eighth century. Ancient Aramaic began around the eleventh century B.C.E. in written form in western Syria. When the Assyrians and Babylonians used transplantation of populations as a way to ensure control over their newly conquered regions, Aramaic became more widespread due to its flexibility and simplicity. When the Persians took control of the entire Near East, their king Darius I made Aramaic the official language of the western Persian Empire. It was at this time that elements of late or classical Aramaic (200 B.C.E. to 1200 C.E.) were used in parts of the books of Ezra and Daniel, making their way into the Bible. By the fourth century B.C.E. Aramaic was the dominant language, although Phoenician was still spoken until the first century B.C.E.

During the New Testament different Aramaic dialects were used in Judea, including Middle Hebrew, Neo-Hebrew, and Hasmonaean Old Judean, which were used side by side for different types of literature. Middle and Neo-Hebrew were descended from the age of the prophets and kings of Israel and continued to be used for theological writings, while Hasmonaean was the written language of Jerusalem and Judea under the Hasmonaeans

(142–37 B.C.E.) and was connected with Jewish independence. Old Judean continued to be used for private writings. The sayings of Jesus were in the Old Judean, indicating that the traditions of Jesus came into Greek not by Galilean Aramaic but rather by way of Jerusalem. There also existed Samaritan and Galilean, dialects of Aramaic used during the time of Jesus. In addition there was an artificial language, the Galilean Targum, which was a mixture of Hasmonaean and the Galilean languages, which was used in the synagogues.[2]

The ancient biblical literature and the Tannaitic (early rabbinic literature) such as the Mishnah show that the Hebrew Bible language is not monolithic. The variations allowed different elements to enter into religious practices from daily life. The Mishnaic or Middle Hebrew used to be seen purely as an artificial scholastic jargon used in theological writings, but modern scholars now view it as a colloquial idiom spoken in the biblical period until 200 C.E. The idea of the Bible being written in one language without other influences must be abandoned. The research in languages shows that the Bible was a living document being influenced by multiple factors.[3]

Latin and Greek

In addition to Aramaic, the major language of the government, merchants, and educated elites was Greek. The major administrative language of the Roman Empire was Latin. A member of the Italic languages of the Indo-European group based its alphabet on Greek. Latin derived from those who migrated into the area around the Tiber in Latium, a tribe called the Latins. Once established, the Latins came into contact with the Etruscans, whose language was non–Indo-European. The Latins inherited the Etruscan alphabet, derived from Greek, which they changed into Latin. An important aspect of ancient or classical Latin was the absence of punctuation and spacing between words. In addition they wrote their letters in capitals. Latin, like its modern Romance Language descendents, did not need word order, like English, and used declensions that provided cases needed to identify the major parts of speech for nouns and pronouns. Thus, the nominative case denoted the subject of a sentence; the genitive case usually showed possession; the accusative was the direct object; the dative showed the indirect object; and the ablative, which showed, among other things, movement to or from someone or something, and was used with prepositions. The final case is the vocative, which was used for direct speech. Although Roman colonists were established throughout the East, Latin was not prominent. Nevertheless, Latin was the official language of the Roman Empire. Pontius Pilate most likely wrote his official correspondences to the emperor and his agents in Latin. Any official pronouncement or legal decisions were also made in Latin. These facts required individuals who knew Latin and the other languages to ensure that documents could be translated and written. But in everyday transactions Latin was not the universal language, Greek was.

Pontius Pilate most likely spoke to the Jewish leaders not in Aramaic, their language, or Latin, his language, but Greek. Classical, or Attic Greek, written by Plato, Aristotle, and Thucydides was not the everyday dialect. The major form of Greek in the Hellenistic Age was *koine*, the common day language of the time. *Koine* was the fusion of Attic or Classical Greek with other Greek dialects. Brought by Alexander the Great's army, *koine* was spread from Egypt to the Indus. The evolution of Greek went from Mycenaean, Ancient or Classical, to Hellenistic or *koine*. One of the earliest Indo-European languages, Greek is attested at least as early as 1200 B.C.E. The ancient Greek alphabet was created around the ninth century B.C.E. The New Testament was written in *koine* Greek, the language of everyday inhabitants.

From the above discussion it is clear that Palestine had a multitude of languages and dialects. This would have impacted daily life in a variety of ways. Individuals would have had to deal with others who spoke different languages, making the area more cosmopolitan. The constant flow of visitors to Jerusalem from the Diaspora would have brought in different views, but it would also potentially bring in prejudices and suspicion. If someone does not speak one's language there is a tendency to mistrust them. In addition there would have been the usual miscommunications that exist between individuals who speak different languages. Another impact would have been relations with authorities. At one level there is the relationship with the Roman administration using Latin and necessitating an understanding of the Roman language. This would be further complicated by the need to understand Roman law and its nuances. At a second level would be the local Jewish authorities who were required to keep the peace. Here the language would be in either Aramaic, if in Jerusalem, or perhaps Greek, if in Herod's court. For the local inhabitants there would be a further issue of which dialect, Samarian, Judean, Galilean, or one of the other subdialects, was being used. There would also be interactions with the old Phoenician cities of Tyre, Sidon, or Byblos. They had their own dialect, which again could complicate the situation.

TARGUM

A peculiar form of literature during the New Testament in Palestine centered on the scriptures read in the synagogues. The scriptures were written in Hebrew, the common language of the kingdom of Israel in 701 B.C.E. (2 Kings 18:26). But after the exile in 587 B.C.E. when Aramaic became the popular language, Hebrew was no longer the common language. By the time of Nehemiah (8:8) Aramaic translations were creeping in. This Aramaic translation became known as the Targum. After the

Hebrew Pentateuch was recited, it was then translated into Aramaic. The Targum was originally oral, but in the Dead Sea Scrolls written examples exist.

Most of the Hebrew Pentateuch translated into Aramaic (the Targum) was done orally, because it was very expensive to have a written copy. This created the situation in which it became hard to know what was original (Hebrew) and what was added, exegesis (interpretation) or gloss (notes originally written in the margin). The latter were in Aramaic. The Pentateuch, called the Torah, not only meant the written law or first five books of the Bible, but also the oral law that included the later written glosses.

The Targum existed within the synagogue with the reading and preaching of the scriptures. The primary goal of the Targumic literature and translation was to make the Hebrew scriptures understandable to the Aramaic-speaking public. These Aramaic translations were known for their popular character, as opposed to the strict, often stilted translation, of the Alexandrian school. The Palestinian Targum attempted to bridge the gap between the authoritative Hebrew and the colloquial Aramaic.

The Targum of the Aramaic Pentateuch as represented in a codex discovered in the Vatican library in 1956 may be descended from an original during the time of Esdras. If so, the Targum was much older than thought and was paralleled with the Hebrew Scriptures during the Hellenistic age and the time of New Testament. The concept of interpretation seen in the Targum also existed in Paul's letters, showing that the Targum influenced not only Judaism but early Christianity as well.

The Targum was not simply a translation. Rather it was an attempt to explain the scriptures for everyday life. Since Hebrew used only consonants, it could be given different vocalizations, which meant that the meaning could change, which therefore opens it up to interpretation. For example *shem*, the word for *name*, could also, with different vowels, mean *sham, there* (Genesis 22:14). The Targum allowed for this interpretation for the Aramaic-speaking public.

The importance of the Targumic literature is that it allowed the general public, whether literate or not, to participate in the synagogue. In the New Testament Jesus is presented as reading the scriptures, Isaiah, and then commenting upon it.

> So he came to Nazareth, where he had been brought up. And as his custom was, he went into the synagogue of the Sabbath day, and stood up to read. And he was handed the book of the prophet Isaiah. And when he had opened the book, he found the place where it was written…Then he closed the book, and gave it back to the attendant and sat down.…And he began to say to them…(Luke 4:16–21)

It would appear from this passage that Jesus read the scripture, probably in Hebrew, and then presented the Targum. The New Testament further shows that early Christianity was connected with Judaism through the

synagogue. Like the liturgy in the synagogue, which continually changed
and helped deal with issues, Christianity used the synagogue and liturgy
to promote their new religion.

Outside of Judea other forms of Aramaic were used, such as Nabataean
in the Arab kingdom of Petra from 400 B.C.E. and Palmyren from 44 B.C.E.
to 274 C.E. Outside the Roman Empire but still of major influence was Ar-
sacid, the language of the Parthian empire, used from 247 B.C.E. to 224 C.E.

INDIVIDUALS AND LANGUAGE

For individuals, such as a farmer, merchant, pilgrim, rabbi, or noble,
some examples might be useful. A farmer living in Galilee would have the
language-dialect Aramaic-Galilean. He would have spent most of his
time in his homestead or village without extensive contact with Roman
officials, and therefore, any official pronouncements by the government
would have reached him only through translations first in Greek then
in Aramaic. This translation may often be inaccurate or not convey the
specific details. For example, in the late empire the Emperor Diocletian
issued a price edict that set a maximum level of goods and service; the
justifications and law were set down in Latin in the preamble to the list of
goods. In Asia Minor a governor attached a letter in Greek to explain the
price edict but in the letter declared that the goods were set at that price,
and not as an upper limit. So even in this instance between the emperor
(or his chancellery) and his governor there is confusion, and in the translation for the general population there is a misreading of the law. In the
daily life of our hypothetical farmer, laws from Rome issued in Latin may
in turn have been translated into Greek, with some changes, and then
into Aramaic with even more changes. Having heard of the new laws or
decree, the farmer may interact with officials, mainly tax collectors, who
may only have known the law from a translated (and perhaps mistrans-
lated) document, causing even more confusion. The farmer would have
had some interaction with nobles or priests at the yearly pilgrimage to
Jerusalem. Since Palestine was small enough to allow travel and communication with various groups, the average farmer would have interacted
with others who used different languages, even if he did not understand
them.

Pilgrims are a special group in that they were not normally interacting
with the local population for extended periods of time. Like the modern
tourist, the pilgrims who visited Palestine during the New Testament period were not necessarily versed in the local language. An Alexandrian
pilgrim would know Greek but probably not Aramaic or Hebrew. His
interaction would have been not with the local population but with religious guides, fellow pilgrims, and those who catered to the traveler, probably conversing in Greek. Pilgrims would often travel together as if in a
modern-day tour group. Some would have known local dialects, and if

not, would have been able to hire a professional guide. Pilgrims would have stayed in hostels, and evidence suggests that these hostels were often associated with synagogues.

A merchant would have more access to other languages and cultures due to his travels. Here a merchant might have as his primary language Greek. This would serve him well in the Roman Empire, and he could travel throughout the lands mentioned in the New Testament without any difficulty. But in his day-to-day dealings with the locals he might have to know the local dialect. There were of course different classes of merchants. Some would have been distributors, in which case knowing the local language would not have been needed as much as for the local retailers, and distributors, who would know Greek to deal with those supplying the goods and Aramaic for their local customers. Many Jewish merchants would have traveled extensively throughout the Mediterranean, which would have allowed them to come into contact with numerous groups, Jewish and gentile. Their travels would have allowed them the opportunity to be exposed to and perhaps learn the different languages. Accounts from Asia Minor have survived showing that merchants made numerous trips to the West. During the first century merchants traveled to and from the East. Unlike earlier periods when the Mediterranean was beset with pirates, making travel dangerous, the first century was a time of general peace. This peace allowed the merchants to have stability and protection.

The rabbis would have spoken Aramaic, and some may have had knowledge of Hebrew. It is unclear if all would have known the language of the Old Testament, and some of the teachers, including Jesus himself, may have been using Aramaic translations or glosses. It is probable that some would have known Greek, although again, we do not know if Jesus had any specific knowledge. It is unlikely that many knew Latin. The rabbis were mainly concerned with the local community, so the most important language for them would have been the local dialect. Those involved in the continual interpretation of the Old Testament would have known Hebrew. The rabbis were the key connection between the local inhabitant and the official religious class in Jerusalem. Although they may not have been nobles, they were trained. The term *rabbi* did not mean a priest necessarily, but it could mean a teacher, someone learned. Jesus is called a rabbi (Matt. 26:25; Mark 9:5; John 1:38, 3:1–3), but it is not clear if he had any formal training. The term could have meant merely someone who had innate intelligence.

The nobles would have had constant contact with the Roman authorities, local Jewish and Greek leaders, and local populations. They would have known Aramaic, Greek, probably Hebrew, and perhaps even Latin. Of all the groups, the nobles would have had the most opportunities to interact with a wide variety of cultures and groups. Their position would have made their access to these different languages quite readily available.

In addition they would have had the opportunities to travel throughout the Mediterranean, interacting with many different groups.

HELLENISM

It is this last group that provides the interaction with the next major component of nonreligious influence, Hellenism. The region of Palestine had numerous influences; chief among them was Hellenism, Greek culture and influence, which occurred after the conquest of Alexander the Great. The Greek influences were initially brought in by soldiers and merchants in Alexander's army, mainly the Macedonians. Although looked down upon by the Athenians and other southern Greeks, the Macedonians were in fact Greek. What made them important was their belief in their own superiority. After defeating the Thebans and forcing the rest of the Greek mainland to submit, the Macedonians then proceeded to conquer the whole of Persia. Fiercely independent and proud, the Macedonians were not willing to blend with the conquered races. Although Alexander attempted to bring Macedonian and Persian together, it never really worked, even in the Seleucid kingdom, which had more occurrences than did the Ptolemies of Egypt. Even here the Greek culture dominated.

The Macedonians thus brought the Greek culture, which they inherited through their domination of Greece, to the conquered lands, which included Palestine and Asia Minor. These regions had already received Greek influences, especially in western Asia Minor. The Macedonians now brought more vigor into the region and most importantly opened up the regions to Greek merchants and colonists. This new avenue allowed Greek culture, fused with other attributes, to produce Hellenism, or Greek-influenced culture, which now took hold.

The indigenous populations did not necessarily accept the new culture. Greek culture really only permeated in the urban areas, and mainly in the recently established Greek cities, and some of the older trade cities. The rural regions and populations, which were considerable, were not easily influenced. Hellenism must then be seen as an urban phenomenon accepted by a small but powerful minority, usually from and for the upper class.

This upper class, however, did not abandon their own native cultures; on the contrary, what seems to have happened was a melding of the two, Greek and local, which produced Hellenistic culture. The local upper class recognized the value in assimilating Greek culture, especially if they wished to profit politically, economically, and socially from their Macedonian masters. But they also kept many of their native customs, even if they did not display them prominently. One area in which they attempted accommodation was language. Learning Greek allowed these individuals to interact more effectively with their political Macedonian masters as well as foreign merchants and traders.

Hellenistic Religious Practices

Language was not the only way locals assimilated Hellenism. Religion became important for some. In Palestine there were pagans in addition to Jews, especially along the coasts and in the deserts. The coastal regions still clung to the ideas of the Philistines and Phoenicians. Worship of the diety Baal continued, which often put them at odds with the Jewish leaders and neighbors. This conflict would often be violent, which further exacerbated the situation, and both sides seemed to agitate this violence. Paganism also existed in the desert regions. Although Judaism made converts and ultimately Herod's family decreed acceptance of Judaism, paganism still remained.

The worship of paganism not only involved prayers to idols and multiple gods but usually required blood sacrifice, that is, sacrificing and eating of animals. Judaism, likewise, had blood sacrifice but only to one God and performed only in the Temple, not other places of worship like the Synagogues. Hellenism introduced new gods, particularly Zeus, Dionysius, and Serapis (a Hellenized Egyptian deity) among others. Although known through variants before, the Macedonians now began to introduce these deities and their worship throughout the region, often forcibly. Temples, often large and grandiose, now dotted the region. During the New Testament time then, paganism existed side by side with Judaism and was seen as a major competitor of Hellenism.

Hellenism was the cultural achievement of the period from the death of Alexander the Great to the defeat of Cleopatra in 30 B.C.E., the Hellenistic Age. Hellenism, however, continued after this period, with the Roman Empire allowing its spread now from the Greek East to the Roman West. The most important center of Hellenism became Alexandria and its great library. Built by Ptolemy I on the foundations laid out by Alexander, the city was exclusively Greek, although located in Egypt. The city attracted scholars and merchants, which allowed it to prosper and become the center for Greek culture. Hellenism was the fusion of this Greek culture with the local cultures. This is perhaps best seen in art and religion.

ART AND RELIGION

Art is an important element of culture. Art allows a society to express its culture. The period of the New Testament resulted in a clash of cultures in art. Jewish art forbade the representation of individuals, especially images of God. This resulted in most Jewish art being centered on geometrical and floral design. In many ways this representation produced a static form of artistic culture. For the non-Jews, there was a rich conglomeration of art. First, there was the ancient Near Eastern culture, seen in Assyrian and Babylonian works. Although they tended to be two-dimensional, the art work represented individuals, both kings and nonroyalty. The major innovation, however, was the introduction of Hellenistic art. This art form brought in the Classical Greek ideas, which were merged with the local influences. One area in which a difference is best seen between Judaism and Hellenistic culture is sculpture.

In Classical and Hellenistic culture, sculpture represented the human and divine. Works highlighted the accomplishments of the gods, as seen in the friezes of the Parthenon. The *Charioteer of Delphi* clearly depicts the facial features of a human. For the Greeks this representation allowed for the worship of the gods or the revering of humans. For the Jews this of course went against the commandment not to have graven images; although the Bible does not condemn sculptures representing humans, the commandment's interpretation extended to living and dead humans. For the Jews during the time of the New Testament this created a dilemma; Jews living both in and out of Palestine were constantly exposed to the sculptures of the time, which represented not only the pagan gods but humans now deified, and for some like Augustus still alive. With this exposure and with Roman dominance the Jews were now forced to realize that their way of life was constantly at odds with the dominant culture. The devout Jew often had to make a decision: observe his religion and potentially insult the authorities or obey the authorities and insult his religion. This clash of cultures could lead to distrust on both sides and often war, such as the Great Jewish War under Nero.

These influences impacted the daily life of individuals throughout the Mediterranean during the time of the New Testament. As a crossroad for cultures Palestine had a variety of languages, which constantly influenced how people reacted and interacted. The different languages allowed for the flow of information and ideas to move through the region. The merchants arriving from distant lands either spoke in the native Aramaic or hoped that the local merchant knew Greek, the international language of trade. But mercantile exchange was not the only interaction. From the letters of Paul and other writers it is apparent that there was a vibrant movement in proselytizing for the different religions, including Judaism, Christianity, and the mystery religions. These interactions using different languages were also influenced by the interactions of different cultures. The most important aspect of these cultural interactions was the interaction between Hellenism and Judaism.

This cultural interaction intersected in religion. For the Greeks, and indeed most pagans, the representation of the gods occurred in human and natural forms. The worship of these representations or cult statues made a connection between the mortal and the divine. These cult statues held special power for a city or region. When one nation defeated another it was not uncommon for the victor to remove the cult statues and take them away where they would then hold them hostage. If the defeated people attempted rebellion, then the cult statue might be destroyed and hence the gods were thought to abandon them. This concept of making the statues "alive" was completely alien to the Jew. Following the second command-ment of not making images of God, the Jews not only resisted the move toward making worldly images, they consistently attempted to destroy all images of the pagan gods. It was in this contact that the Hellenistic and Jewish cultures mingled, often with violent results.

NOTES

1. Gary A. Rendsburg, "Semitic Languages," in *Near Eastern Archaeology: A Reader,* ed. Suzanne Richard, pp. 71–73 (Winona Lake, IN: Eisenbrauns, 2003).

2. Klaus Beyer, *The Aramaic Language and Its Distribution and Subdivisions,* trans. John F. Healey (Gottingen: Vandenhoeck and Ruprecht, 1986).

3. Richard C. Steiner, "Ancient Hebrew," in *The Semitic Languages,* ed. Robert Hetron, pp. 145–73 (London: Routledge, 1997).

4

PRE-MESSIANIC JUDAISM: WORSHIP AND TEMPLE PRACTICES

Then as he went out of the Temple, one of his disciples said to him "Teacher, see what manner of stones and what buildings are here!" And Jesus answered and said to him "Do you see these great buildings? Not one stone shall be left upon another, that shall not be thrown down." (Mark 13:1–3)

JEWISH TEMPLE

Since the days of Solomon, Jewish life had focused on the Temple and the religious worship in the city of Jerusalem. After its destruction and the Babylonian captivity, religious practices changed. During this time the synagogue arose to allow the continuation of Judaism in the absence of the Temple. When Herod the Great rebuilt the Temple it had the same general plan as Solomon's. Interestingly, the New Testament does not provide much information about the Temple; however, the Jewish historian Josephus does provides a description of the Temple complex with some further information coming from the Talmud.

The Temple was an imposing structure dominating the whole of Jerusalem, as recorded in the Gospel of Mark. Built on a series of terraces, the courts grew in importance in terms of their arrangement, with the Temple being the highest. The whole complex, according to Josephus, was one stadium, or about 630 feet, while the Talmud indicated it was 500 cubits, or about 700 feet.[1] The structure dominated Jerusalem and was the crowning

Model of Herod's Temple as it appeared in 30 B.C.E. Courtesy of Library of Congress.

architectural achievement of Herod for the city. The Temple was not only a glorification of Herod's rule, but more importantly was a glorification of Judaism, which would allow his nation to compete in Greek society. For the common person, the Temple was the focal point of religion, nation, and pride.

Surrounding the Temple complex were walls with gates that controlled the passage into the complex to not only ensure safety but to allow for crowd control. On the inside the walls had double porticoes on three sides and a triple on the south side. These porticoes ensured comfort from the direct sun and inclement weather. With roofs of cedar, 25 cubits high, they contained mosaic pavements that allowed for access to the court of the gentiles on either side of the central Temple structure. As one approached the inner Temple area, a warning wall with an inscription warned gentiles and those unclean not to enter. On the east side one entered from the E gate or Nicanor's gate, made of Corinthian brass, which had a height of 40 cubits, was richly adorned, and was the central and most important entrance to the Temple. Here, the court of the women, a square of 135 cubits, was surrounded by walls with porticoes, and at the corners were rooms used to store wood unfit for the altar sacrifices, for lepers to wash themselves, for storage of wine and oil, and for the Nazirites (men who had taken special vows) to shave their hair and cook the animal flesh that had been sacrificed. Going through the women's court, one entered the court of the Israelites or the men's court. This area measured 187 by 135 cubits and surrounded the Temple proper. Along the walls were storage rooms for utensils used in the Temple. On the eastern side there was a narrow court of 11 cubits, which was the court of the priests and where stood the

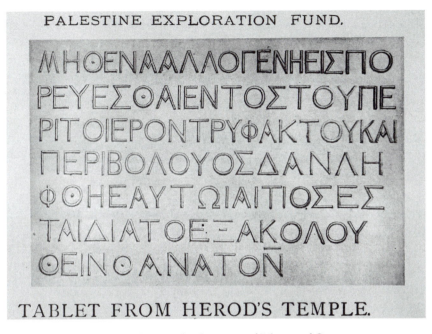

PALESTINE EXPLORATION FUND.

TABLET FROM HEROD'S TEMPLE.

A tablet taken from Herod's Temple. Courtesy of Library of Congress.

altar where the burnt offerings were made; moving further west on the high platform stood the Temple proper.

One climbed 12 stairs to approach the Temple proper, which had a length and height of a 100 cubits. One entered through the porch into the Holy Place, which was 40 cubits long, 20 wide and 60 high, where were located one golden lamp, a table for bread representing the presence of God, and an altar for incense. A wooden partition was between the Holy Place and the Holy of Holies, which was 20 cubits long and was empty since the Ark of the Covenant no longer existed. A veil existed between these two rooms and was probably the veil mentioned in the Gospel narrative, which was ripped at Jesus' death, because if it had been totally inside the Holy of Holies no one would have seen it because only the High Priest could enter there.

FORTRESS ANTONIA

The entire Temple complex was a series of platforms rising up, which became one of the highest structures in Jerusalem and could be seen from the surrounding area; on the southwest corner stood the Antonia Fortress, which was slightly higher. This fortress built by Herod and named for Marc Antony provided security for the city. Herod's construction, especially its height, caused many of the Jews, in particular the religious

TABLET FROM HEROD'S TEMPLE.
_____

/ It is one of those tablets which forbade strangers, as Josephus tells us, from passing the sacred enclosure. The translation is :—

" No stranger is to enter within the balustrade round the temple and enclosure. Whoever is caught will be responsible to himself for his death, which will ensue."

The passage of Josephus is as follows :—

" When you go through these first cloisters unto the second (court of the seven temples), there was a partition made of stone all round, whose height was three cubits ; its construction was very elegant. Upon it stood pillars at equal distances from one another, declaring the laws of purity, some in Greek, and some in Roman letters, that no ' foreigner should go within that sanctuary.' "

Tablet translation from Herod's Temple. Courtesy of Library of Congress.

leaders, to resent Herod. The fortress provided the city with security, but it also resulted in a heightened tension. The fortress became the symbol of oppression, first from Herod and then Rome. Rome used the fortress to ensure dominance and peace. Unfortunately it was a double-edged sword. While it symbolized the Roman domination and allowed them to control the city, it became the symbol of oppression and the center of opposition. The local Jews viewed it as foreign and its presence prompted protests. These protests could lead to violence and potential rebellion. The fortress became the flash-point during the events leading up to the great rebellion. The garrison was trapped and forced to endure humiliation when it surrendered after a siege.

TABERNACLE

In the interior of the Temple stood the Tabernacle, or the Sanctuary, where God dwelled. In the original Temple built by Solomon, the Tabernacle contained the Ark of the Covenant. The Tabernacle had an outer court and an inner sanctum, the Holy of Holies, separated by a curtain or veil. The outer court had the menorah, pictured on the Arch of Titus, a table for the loaves of bread, and an altar where incense was burned. Passing through this inner veil or curtain one entered the Holy of Holies or *kodesh*, which during the time of Herod's remodeling of the Second Temple (here called Herod's Temple) was empty since the Ark of the Covenant had disappeared after Solomon. The menorah became the most recognized symbol of the Jewish state and religion. Said to symbolize the burning bush where God spoke to Moses on Mount Sinai (Exodus 25), the menorah was used in the Tabernacle before the Temple was built and later placed in the outer court in the Temple. Beaten from a single piece of gold (Exodus 25:3–40), the menorah was fueled by olive oil located at each end of the seven branches. The theory as to its origins is debated. One holds that it comes from a plant with seven branches growing in the desert, while another has it coming from the seven cosmological bodies known at the time: sun, moon, Mercury, Venus, Mars, Jupiter, and Saturn. A final idea comes from the ancient Sumerian ideology of the mother goddess, which was later changed into a representation of monotheism. It is impossible to determine which one, if any at all, are the basis of its origin.

The menorah was represented on coins and became associated with the feast of Hanukkah, when the Temple was desecrated and miraculously the oil left in the menorah continued to burn without refilling for eight days until new consecrated oil could be brought into the rebuilt consecrated Temple. After the destruction of the Temple in 70 c.e., the Romans removed the menorah from Jerusalem and brought it back to Rome in triumph, where it was placed in the Temple of Peace built by the Emperor Vespasian, father of the conquering general Titus, and remained until the Vandals sacked the city in 455 c.e. The Vandals removed the menorah to Carthage, where it remained until General Belisarius from the Eastern Empire under Justinian conquered the city and removed it to Constantinople. The writer Procopius, a contemporary of Belisarius, stated that it was brought in triumph through the streets of the Eastern capital. He then stated that it was sent back to Jerusalem, although no other evidence exists for this statement. After this episode the menorah was lost.

The Tabernacle and its outlines became the blueprint for the synagogues, where the ark in the front contains the Torah and is the holiest part of the structure, similar to the Ark of the Covenant, which contained the Ten Commandments in the Holy of Holies. The synagogue, especially in modern society, contains the menorah and a raised platform where the Torah is read, akin to the ancient menorah and the altar.

SYNAGOGUE

The synagogue traces its origin to the period of the Exile after the destruction of Solomon's Temple and the Babylonian Captivity. Since they were without contact with Jerusalem and the sacred site, the Jewish leaders began the process of formalizing the rituals without the need for the Temple. The leaders realized that with the dispersion of Jews, both before and after the destruction of the Temple, Judaism was in danger of being obliterated. The leaders therefore developed the plans for individual worship places, the forerunners of the synagogues. The synagogues would face Jerusalem.

The synagogue, *beit ha-knesset,* means "assembly house" and comes from the Greek word meaning "to gather." The synagogue has a large sanctuary where the prayers are performed. Although their exact date of origin is unknown, they were common by the first century c.e., mentioned by the writers Josephus and Philo, the New Testament, and rabbinic sources. An inscription from Jerusalem has the following message:

> Theodotos, son of Vettenos the priest and synagogue leader, son of a synagogue leader and grandson of a synagogue leader, built the synagogue for the reading of the Torah and studying of the commandments and as a hostel with chambers and water installation to provide for the needs of itinerants from abroad, which his fathers, the elders, and Simonides founded.[2]

Clearly even in Jerusalem, during the time of the Temple, a synagogue existed, used not only for prayer but as a hostel or hotel. The synagogue then may be seen not only as a center of worship but as a place of hospitality. This meant that the function of synagogues extended beyond the actual building. It is feasible to assume that the structure may not have been the only part of the complex. The quoted inscription may point to the idea that attached to the place of worship, what we call the synagogue, was a hostel or guest house. This idea may be seen in later Christian structures such as monasteries and abbeys, which had guest houses attached to them.

In the Talmud, Toefta Megillach 3:21–23 said that the synagogue, like the Temple, should be on the highest point of the town, doors opening to the east. The interior was to be directed toward the Teva or Scroll box on a wall aligned with Jerusalem. The elders were to sit facing the people with their backs to the *qodesh* (Jerusalem), the Teva faces the people with the back to *qodesh,* and the people face the *qodesh.*

But synagogues were not all based on a standard outline. There were three major types that which archaeologists have now classified from the more than 100 synagogues known from antiquity in Palestine. There is the broad house, where the walls have an orientation in which one is longer or Broader, with the Torah shrine on the broad wall aligned with Jerusalem. The longhouse consisted of an atrium, with the Torah shrine on a platform on the Jerusalem-aligned wall. The Torah shrine, called the *arona,* was flanked by a seven-branched menorah. Later, over an apse on the Jerusalem wall there was sometimes a screen that separated it from the rest of the interior. The third type was the Galilean, found at Capernaum from the second or third century c.e. It was a monumental synagogue not seen elsewhere and had a -U shaped arrangement of columns inside the synagogue.

In the New Testament Jesus not only attended the synagogue (Matt. 12:9; Luke 4:44) but was allowed to read aloud the passages from the Old Testament, which not only included the Torah but other works as well, such as the book of Isaiah (Luke 4:16–22). After reading the passage Jesus expounded or taught about the selected reading, giving a homily. The synagogue then acted as a connection between the old and the new. The synagogue with its orientation toward the Temple allowed the Judaism of the Old Testament, before the Exile, to connect with the new reality of Judaism spreading beyond its traditional borders. In the letters of Paul and the Acts of the Apostles it is clear that Paul spoke in the synagogues (Acts 13:5, 15, 14:1). His attempt was to first bring the new religion to Jews and then to move beyond them and convert Gentiles.

Synagogues in Rome

Synagogues have been found in numerous cities in the east but are also known to have existed in Rome. The early Christians in Rome who witnessed with Peter and Paul must have had contact with the Jewish synagogues. When Peter arrived in the city in the 40s, he naturally would have used his Jewish ancestry and tradition to begin his missionary activity in Rome. During this time there were probably five synagogues in Rome; one, the Synagogue of the Hebrews, had existed since the late republic, while two others were established during the reign of Augustus, honoring him and his son-in-law Marcus Agrippa. A fourth synagogue honored Herod the Great and was probably also built during Augustus's time. A fifth synagogue may have honored a tribune in Syria, Volumnius, and a patron of the Jews. These synagogues were located across the Tiber region in Region 14, which is modern Trastevere. This quarter was known to have housed a large number of immigrants, especially those who worked on the Tiber loading and unloading barges.

Although no archaeological remains exist of the ancient synagogues in Rome, nearby in Ostia, Rome's port, a first-century synagogue has been discovered and excavated. This building was originally built as a synagogue, as opposed to other sites, even those in Rome, which seem to have originally been private houses and then turned into synagogues.

JEWISH ART

Throughout its history Judaism had a strict observance concerning art. Jewish art was created specifically for the Jewish community according to the specific laws. The art of the Second Temple was decorative, characterized by nature. Unlike the Hellenistic art, which commemorated the individual, Jewish art was formed of floral, geometric, and architectural patterns. The art avoided representations of people and most importantly did not make any representation of God. These restrictions were made due to the interpretation of the Commandment forbidding graven images. Judaism did not allow sculptures or representations of images in the heavens and on earth. Josephus mentions the destruction of Herod Antipas's palace by the mob because it was decorated with animal figures. After the destruction of the Temple Jewish art continued in the synagogue, but by the end of the second century C.E. figurative art developed. Here biblical scenes, the zodiac cycle, and the traditional flora, geometric, and architectural patterns were seen.[3]

SACRIFICES AND CELEBRATIONS

An important element in the Temple complex and in Jewish society was the sacrifice. The Temple had morning and afternoon offerings in which prayers were recited such as the Barchu, the Shema, and the Priestly Blessing. During these prayer services Psalms were recited. These daily sacrifices were then augmented with the offerings on the Sabbath and the Jewish holidays.

The offerings, the *korban* (plural *korbanot*), meaning sacrifice, were performed by the *kohanim* (singular *kohen*), the Jewish priests, in the Temple. The sacrifice honored Yahweh and was a sign of the compact or covenant between God and the Jews. The sacrifice was usually an animal, justified in the story of God's acceptance of Abel's offering of a lamb over his brother's Cain offering of fruits and vegetables. The animal was ritually killed and then cooked over the fire as a fulfillment of the Jewish part of the compact. The animal could be a bull or sheep, and some cooked parts were eaten by the priests while others were allowed to burn (eaten by God). It is probable that the sacrifice of sheep and bulls was reserved for the wealthy or for special occasions, because the *korbanot* could also include doves, grain, incense, and other materials.

With the destruction of Jerusalem in 70 C.E., the Temple was not only destroyed but the concept of the sacrifice vanished as well. Because the Romans forbade the reconstruction of the Temple, the practice of Jewish sacrifice ended. At this point the synagogue took on even more of an important role. The structure now became the center of Jewish religion. Here the Pharisees were triumphant over the Sadducees and the Temple rituals.

The Temple sacrifices were performed by the *kohen* or priest. The priests were male descendents of Aaron, Moses's brother, who had specific qualifications. Since Aaron was of the tribe of Levi, all priests were Levites. Being a member of the tribe of Levi, however, did not automatically make one a priest. Those who did not become priests could help out in the Temple and provide support, including being Temple guards, workmen, and assistants. The *kohanim* began their duties as the age of 20 and continued in service until 60, when they retired. The individual wishing to be a priest had to meet certain qualifications in addition to being a Levite, male, and 20 years old. They could not have any physical liabilities such as blindness, leprosy, lameness, cataracts, and others (a full list is given in Leviticus 21:18–20). The idea behind these limitations was to ensure that the Temple was not polluted with impurities. The priests received their maintenance and rewards from the Temple gifts such as food, clothing, and even property.

Rules were imposed on the *kohanim* to prevent their ritual defilement. For example, the *kohen* could not come into contact with corpses, including in the customary mourning rites, except for their nearest relatives: father, mother, brother, and so on. This even extended to entering a house or building with a corpse, or even a cemetery. The priest could not marry a divorcee, a convert, or of course a prostitute. If a priest married one of these individuals the marriage was still valid and the children were legitimate, but they could no longer be priests. The high priest could only marry a virgin.

One priest became the high priest or the *kohen gadol*. His primary job was to oversee the Yom Kippur service. During the time of Herod the Great and the Romans, the High Priest became more of a political appointment to ensure smooth running of the Jewish state and the secular authorities. The high priest owed his position to an outside force. The office of high priest was now co-opted and the high priest became a puppet of the secular state. Some may have even viewed the position as a corruption of their religion. This view may have even given many of the Zealots an argument for retribution against the high priests as collaborators.

The Temple and the functions of the priestly class centered on the great Jewish festivals or feasts, of which there were seven. These feasts were both religious and agricultural, that is, they were centered on the religious heritage of the Jewish experience but held during seasons of agricultural life. The first, the Passover or Pesach, is celebrated in spring on the 14th day of the first month and begins the Jewish religious calendar. Its agricultural importance was that it began the harvest season. It is possible that the early celebration of this part of the feast came from an earlier pre-Jewish festival centered on the agricultural life of society. The major emphasis, however, during the historical period, was its commemoration of independence. The Passover celebrated the deliverance of the Jews from Egypt (Exodus 11–14). The feast celebrated the "passing over" of the angel of death, when the Jews spread lambs' blood over the doorpost so that the first born son was not killed. Associated with this feast is the Fast of the Firstborn, celebrated the day before Passover, when firstborn males fast in celebration of their safety when the last plague visited Egypt. The Passover also celebrates the general deliverance of the Jews from Egypt by crossing the Red Sea. For seven days after Passover, the Feast of Unleavened Bread, where matzah or bread without leaven is used (Exodus 12:15–28) is celebrated. Associated with Passover, this festival is again meant to show how the Jews had to make haste in their fleeing Egypt and ensuring their safety. Finally, on the last day of the Feast of Unleavened Bread the celebration of the First Fruits occurs. Here, the Jews took to the Temple the first-born animal, first cuts of barley and wheat, and first fruits. These three festivals celebrated the religious struggles of Jewish freedom from their Egyptian masters.

The fourth great celebration was Pentecost or Shavuot, when the Jews celebrated Moses receiving the Ten Commandments on Mount Sinai from God 50 days after Passover (Exodus 19–20). The celebration also occurred during the harvest of wheat. Again it probably had its origin in an earlier agricultural feast that was taken over for religious purposes for the new monotheistic religion.

The fifth festival is Rosh Hashanah or the Feast of the Trumpets (Leviticus 23:23–25), which begins the civil New Year on the first day of the seventh month, either September or October. It is the beginning of 10 days of penance ending with the Day of Atonement or Yom Kippur, the sixth festival. Yom Kippur or the Day of Atonement is the most sacred day of the Jewish calendar. It was the only day that the High Priest could enter the Holy of Holies to make atonement for the Jewish people.

The final feast is the Festival of the Tabernacles (Sukkot). Again it had its origin in the agricultural cycle and it reminds the Jews of their time wandering in the desert. It is the last celebration and occurs five days after Yom Kippur. It is a time of celebration and joy lasting for seven days.

These festivals mainly commemorate the passage from Egypt and the wandering in the desert. But they also contain hints as to their earlier history and meaning, that of agriculture. Like so many religions, Judaism attempted to bring together traditional festivals common to rural life, such as planting and harvesting, with religious ideology. In so doing the agricultural component eventually disappeared, superseded by religious ideology.

During the time of the New Testament these festivals were celebrated. The Gospels make mention of the Passover and the Feast of Pentecost. In the later works of the New Testament the festivals are not as pronounced because the works tended to deal either with groups that did not have a strong or any Jewish connection or dealt with local dissensions. The Gospels, however, clearly place some emphasis on the great feast of Passover. For it was at this feast period that Jesus was executed and according to his followers rose from the dead.

ASTROLOGY AND MAGIC

Although Judaism was associated with monotheism, other forces influenced Jewish society and perception. Because Judaism arose in the East and was Semitic, other forces in the region influenced the religion and foreign perception. One of these was magic and with it astrology. Jews were often lumped together with sorcerers and magicians in the New Testament time. In the Acts of the Apostles a magician from Samania, Simon, attempted to purchase the powers of Christ from Peter, giving rise to the sin of simony, buying of Church powers (Acts 8:9–24). The passage indicates that Simon was a popular magician who was seen as having powers. His perception of buying the powers of Christ must not have been seen as outrageous by the non-Jews because Simon does not appear to have questioned the legitimacy of the powers, he merely wished to obtain them.

The power and influence of magic should not be underestimated. There are numerous papyri that have magical potions, curses, and charms existing from the ancient period. Some of these potions were said to be in the hands of learned Jews, such as Maria the Jewess, who supposedly had knowledge of alchemy, the ability to turn base metals into gold. Her reputation spread throughout Egypt during the third century C.E., and magic texts claiming her ability were spread far and wide. Some of the popular charms and curses were meant either to either harm or protect individuals.

The New Testament also mentions astrologers, known more colloquially as "wise men." These individuals, mentioned in the Gospel of Matthew, were not Jews but magi or astrologers from the East, although their exact place of origin is not stated. Their visit, first to the court of Herod the Great and then to Jesus, Mary, and Joseph, is again treated as merely a matter of fact. They reported that they had witnessed and traced the path of a star (cosmic body) and consulted their charts. The story, which may not be true, nevertheless related material that would not have aroused suspicion by the reader. These wise men or magi were then seen as everyday occurrences. Judaism did not condone the use of magic or astrology, but other Near Eastern societies advocated and used it (Matt. 2:1–12). But why would the Gospel of Matthew mention this event? While part of it was to place Jesus' birth in Bethlehem, it may have also been used as a message to non-Jews in Palestine. Because the region was full of different cultures and religions, this story allowed the message of Christianity to be accepted by non-Jewish individuals.

Privately many Jews used magic and astrology and looked for magic to protect them. Amulets continued to be popular. For many they held powers. Whether these powers came from some sort of psychological belief or superstition is immaterial; what was important for the individual was that the amulet allowed the individual to feel protected. In addition to amulets, other forms of magic existed. Another important mechanism was the spell. They could be used for both good and evil. For example they were used to save or protect someone. Through the utterance of certain words in a particular order and using a systematic order of sequence, the individual would be safe. Another positive spell might be for having children. On the other hand, spells could be used for malevolent purposes. Spells exist that are meant to destroy someone. For example there are spells that are to cause a former lover to have pain, or an opponent in love or in life to die. Privately then, the use of magic and astrology existed and was used to help soothe people's minds.

Associated with magic and astrology was medicine. Jews, in particular female Jews, were famous for their use of medicines and herbs. Learning from other cultures with which they constantly came into contact, Jewish medicine became prized throughout the Mediterranean. This of course produced not only admiration but scorn. Desired by many wealthy and powerful individuals, Jews knowledgeable about medicine, who could alleviate pain and suffering, could quickly attain power and prestige. But this newfound power opened them up to attacks. Because Jews were easily identifiable they were open to attack. A successful Jewish doctor could easily be identified as a magician or sorcerer, which opened them up to legal and public attack. In this capacity Roman law helped the accuser and Roman public opinion only strengthened the case against Jews.

For the Romans the use of magic and astrology was officially banned, but privately it was used and endorsed as in other cultures. Although the Roman state traditionally viewed the Near Eastern practice with distrust, many Romans, rich and poor, powerful and common, used magic and astrology. One such individual was the Emperor Tiberius, who had his own private astrologer, even though he banned them, along with Jews, from Rome and Italy. This seemingly hypocritical position is best understood in the changing movements in the Mediterranean during the Roman period. On the official side, the old conservative Roman West viewed magic and astrology as dangerous, orgiastic, out of control, and subversive; but on the private side the individual desired to know the future, or how to ensure love, happiness, or wealth, or how to curse and destroy an enemy. These individual desires transcended all societies because they struck at the core of humanity. Roman officials could expel astrologers but then keep them privately around.

Jews were then lumped into these roles not only because of their geographic position in the Near East, but also because of their knowledge of medicine. Because some medicines were made with herbs and drugs, this sometimes produced suspicion of magic, especially if the treatment included prayers or sayings.

BIOGRAPHY OF CAIAPHAS

Caiaphas, high priest during the time of Jesus, held the office longer than any other high priest during the first century c.e. His full name was Joseph bar Caiaphas, but he was simply known as Caiaphas; he had been installed as high priest in 18 c.e. by Valerius Gratus, the procurator or governor of Judea who preceded Pontius Pilate (26–36 c.e.). He maintained his power from 18 to 37 c.e. and seemingly had a close relationship with both Gratus and Pilate. Caiaphas was the son-in-law of Annas, the high priest from 6–15 c.e. Annas appears to have continued to exert influence and in the Gospel of Luke was named high priest alongside Caiaphas, even though Caiaphas was the real high priest. Caiaphas as high priest lived in the Upper City of Jerusalem.

It is conceivable that he supported the Sadducees and may have been part of an embassy to Rome in 17 c.e. When he became high priest he was president of the Sanhedrin or the Great Assembly. During his rule Jesus was brought before him and the Sanhedrin, where he was accused of impiety and ultimately treason. In 36 Pilate was removed by the governor of Syria, Vitellius, and during the Passover of 37 Caiaphas was likewise removed by Vitellius.

The close workings of Caiaphas and the Roman procurators, Gratus and Pilate, may have resulted in a general feeling of uneasiness among the populace. This uneasiness may have ultimately forced the Romans to recall Pilate and dismiss Caiaphas in the hope of winning popular support.

In 1990 archaeologists discovered the Caiaphas family tomb containing 12 ossuaries, one of which had the name in Aramaic, Joseph son of Caiaphas. The remains contained the bones of a 60-year-old man, a woman, two children, and two infants.

NOTES

1. *Herod's Temple Illustration,* http://www.bible-history.com/jewishtemple/ JEWISH_TEMPLEHerods_Temple_Illustration.htm.

2. Steven Fine, "Synagogues in the Land of Israel," in *Near Eastern Archaeology: A Reader,* ed. Suzanne Richard, pp. 455–64 (Winona Lake, IN: Eisenbrauns, 2003), p. 455.

3. Rachel Hachlili, "Jewish Art and Iconography in the Land of Israel," in *Near Eastern Archaeology: A Reader,* ed. Suzanne Richard, pp. 445–54 (Winona Lake, IN: Eisenbrauns, 2003).

5

EXPECTATIONS OF THE MESSIAH

Who do men say that I, the Son of Man, am?...He said to them, But who do you say that I am? Simon Peter answered and said, You are the Christ, the Son of the living God. Jesus answered and said to him, Blessed are you, Simon Bar-Jonah, for flesh and blood has not revealed this to you, but My Father who is in heaven. (Matt. 16:13–17)

DIFFERENT MESSIAHS

The New Testament is the story of the Messiah and his coming. While Christians accept Jesus as the true Messiah, he was not the only one who proclaimed himself Messiah, which means "Anointed One." The importance of the Messiah in Judaism cannot be underestimated. Promised since the beginning of Judaism, the person of the Messiah took on different focuses depending on the situation. He was to be a religious, political, or military leader or a combination of them.

The New Testament Messiah is presented as a religious savior, someone who would fulfill the promise and prophecy of the Old Testament to bring salvation to the Jews. The problem with the prophecy was that it was not clear when the Messiah would come and what he would do to bring about this salvation. With Judea occupied throughout its recent history, a political hope was often paramount. But in the New Testament Jesus is heralded as the "Son of God," the "Anointed One," or the "Prince of Peace." Jesus' message was simple: he was the son of God who had arrived to forgive sins and therefore lead the Jewish people to salvation. In the New Testament he clearly did not have a violent political program, and in many ways the New Testament preached accommodations with the Romans. For example, Jesus was asked if it was acceptable to pay taxes to Rome (Matt. 22:16–21). The implication of the question was if he had said no, than he was preaching rebellion and would have been arrested for treason; but if he said yes, he would have been seen as a collaborator and possibly left himself open to attacks. Jesus of course preached that one has to obey the civil laws but also give God his due. Jesus therefore did not preach rebellion. Even when Pontius Pilate, the Roman governor, had him tried and ultimately convicted of treason, the image in the New Testament is that Pilate did it out of reluctance. Having said this, it must be remembered that the New Testament was written well after Jesus' death and by his followers or even their followers. In other words, Jesus' own message may have changed due to the political realities after the Jewish rebellion. Although his message probably was one of peace, he may have included anti-Roman feelings now and then that were then omitted once Christians attempted to identify themselves as separate from the Jewish rebellion.

But the image of Jesus portrayed in the New Testament was not the only image of the Messiah. Many hoped he would be a political figure, a successor to the Maccabees. Some hoped that the Messiah would restore Israel to its former political glory, not just the Maccabean state but the kingdom of David and Solomon when Israel was an important political and military power in the Near East. This image of the Messiah would be a royal king, a descendent from the house of David. This image was so strong that after the destruction of Jerusalem during the Great Jewish War, all descendents from the house of David were ordered hunted down by the Emperor Domitian (80–96 C.E.). Even Jesus was viewed in some ways as this type of Messiah. Said to be from the house of David, he would inherit the kingship in Judea. This fear of a king supposedly prompted Herod the Great with attempting to slaughter the innocents (probably un-true), and forced Pontius Pilate to deal with Jesus at his trial as a usurper and therefore convict him.

In many ways the image of a political savior was foremost in the Jewish mind. Jesus may in fact have viewed himself in this light, and the image may have been changed by his followers after his death. The epitaphs given to Jesus: "Son of God," "Prince of Peace," and the references to the "Kingdom of Heaven" point to a political concept as well as a spiritual image. This political image required that the savior be a king, and this ultimately forced Rome to take any talk of kings and kingdoms seriously. One thing Rome feared was a military uprising.

The military leader was a common image of the Messiah during the New Testament period. Individuals who could rebel and throw Rome out of Judea were popular, even if not publicly supported. Since Rome was a foreign pagan ruler, any talk of restoring Israel's independence was popular. There were numerous individuals who proclaimed themselves as the Messiah and attempted armed rebellion. Their defeat and executions quickly ended their position as the Messiah. Although Jesus did not preach this form of the Messiah, many hoped he would incite a rebellion. One of his followers was called Simon the Zealot, the Zealots being a group which argued for a military Messiah.

The ultimate hope of a military Messiah would occur during the Great Jewish War of 66–69 C.E. During this war it was prophesied by some that a military leader would destroy the Romans and restore the Jewish kingdom of David. Many assumed that when the war broke out God would wreak his vengeance upon the Romans by destroying their armies without any Jewish casualties. This of course did not happen. Even with the defeat of most of its armies and the destruction of Jerusalem some held out in the fortress at Masada, but eventually they too were defeated.

THE GREAT JEWISH WAR

The rebellion, regardless of its origin, soon took on a colossal struggle between Judaism and paganism, nationalism and foreign imperialism, light and darkness, freedom and slavery. The Jewish rebels hoped that against all odds they would militarily defeat Rome just as their ancestors had against the Syrians nearly three centuries earlier. The struggle affected all lines of Judaism. The military conflict, hoping that a military Messiah would deliver them, drastically changed the daily life of all Palestine. This change pushed the society from a "peaceful" existence to a military footing. All of society, whether or not they wished for a military Messiah, was now caught up in it. The war devastated Judea. Towns were destroyed; fields were ruined; individuals were killed, enslaved, or made refugees, producing a heavy toll on society. In crushing the rebellion Rome cared not about a negative press, which probably did not extend far, but rather desired to ensure that the region did not break away. For the local inhabitants life became a series of trials and hardship.

A hypothetical situation can be imagined and created. An older women and wife has three married sons in their twenties with children, and two daughters, one married, the youngest not, in their teens. Her husband joins the rank of rebels, together with two of her sons. At first the Jewish rebels defeat the small Roman force which in turn emboldens them and they now begin to fortify the northern regions. With the arrival of the Roman commander Vespasian with the eastern army, the rebels are pushed into a town where they are besieged. The woman, with her remaining son, her grandchildren, and her unmarried daughter flee south to her parents' farmstead. News now reaches her that the town her husband and two sons took refuge in has fallen to the Romans. She does not know if they have died, fled, or been enslaved. Unable to return north because the Romans have occupied the region, she has no idea if her daughter and her family are safe. With the Romans moving south, the woman now abandons her farm and her parents and flees to Jerusalem. Here the city is soon overrun by more refugees, and when the Romans finally arrive and besiege the city it is hopeless. In the end the woman sees her youngest son killed, her grandchildren starved, her daughter enslaved and bound for Rome, and she is left destitute without any knowledge of her family's future. The ravages of war produced real hardships that completely destroyed society. And for the Jews, the final insult was that the old Temple tax now became the Jewish tax.

The military defeat in the first Jewish Rebellion and in the second, or Bar Kochba War, ended all hope for a military/political Messiah. These defeats prompted the Christian sect to further separate from Judaism and now view the Messiah, whom they identified as Jesus, less in political/military connotations and more as a religious leader. The Messiah became less of a national-societal image and more of a personal savior. The Messiah did not propose a political-geographical kingdom but rather a spiritual princedom, heaven. It was the military defeat during the Jewish rebellion that ultimately made the Messiah a religious figure.

IMAGES OF THE MESSIAH

But why was there a major difference in the expectations of a Messiah? Why did the first centuries B.C.E and C.E. produce these different images? One reason was the political situation. With the loss of Jewish independence, first during Herod's rule and then under Roman control, there was the hope that someone would save Israel from foreign occupation. Jewish resentment of Roman paganism also played into the expectation about the Messiah. A savior would arrive who would push the pagans out of Judea.

The political climate was not the only reason for the different messianic views. Hellenism produced different messages in Judaism. While some groups welcomed or at least tolerated Hellenism, others regarded the intrusion of Greek culture as an attack on Judaism and its unique position in the Near East. This situation produced a struggle between those who wanted to purge the state of foreign, that is, Greek, elements, and those who sought accommodations within the wider Roman Empire. The Messiah for some would promote a pure form of Judaism. The messianic prophecies also produced a situation in which traditional Judaism had to deal with recent converts. The best example centered in Galilee. Looked down upon as a region of "country bumpkins," Galilee became known for its particular brand of Judaism, one not following the Temple in all matters. Interestingly the most nationalist ideas about the Messiah came from Galilee.

The different forms of the expected Messiah produced different sects that argued for specific ideas. These sects, or perhaps it is better to say philosophies, each had their own agenda and tenets.

Sadducees

Traditional Judaism, or rather the group closely associated with the Temple, was identified with the Sadducee party. The Sadducees positioned themselves as the guardians of the Temple and its rituals and believed in the written law, that of the Pentateuch and other written scriptures. Although occasionally said to be only in favor of the Torah, that is a misrepresentation, as it was the Samaritans who believed only in the Pentateuch. They did, however, believe that there would be no change in the law. In other words they did not believe in adapting to the changing social and economic conditions of the age. They may have originally been from the countryside, which would have fit with their conservative views. Rural societies and individuals usually do not advocate change, they believe in the status quo, and the Sadducees fit this profile. It is possible that they accumulated power and wealth by increasing their land holdings and then translating that into political power by backing the Hasmonean dynasty. Although not really a sect, they believed in the continuation of the status quo, because their power was derived from the Temple. The Sadducees argued against the resurrection of the body. As seen in the Gospels, they were a conservative group and were against Hellenism. As conservative anti-Hellenists the Sadducees consisted mainly of wealthy and well-educated Jews who believed and argued for their own national identity.

Pharisees

The group or party that differed with the Sadducees was the Pharisees, whose name means separated for a life of purity and piousness. They argued for adherence to the rules of Moses but differed from the Sadducees in several important ways. First, they argued in favor of the resurrection of the body. Unlike the Sadducees, who believed that the body simply decayed, similar to the Greek ideology, the Pharisees believed that the body would ultimately resurrect. A second way in which the Pharisees differed was their attitude toward proselytizing. The Pharisees viewed the world as a place for missionary activity, whereas the Sadducees believed in a more traditional ethnic view of Judaism. The Pharisees realized that in order for Judaism to survive and prosper they would have to go out into the Hellenized world. The Pharisees made and changed the laws to fit the new environment. They may have been originally from the urban area and so appealed to the people and saw the need for change. They became the people's party and were the dominant group.

The two would compete not only religiously but socially, politically, and economically. The Sadducees, however, being conservative, relied on the written law as their authority without advocating change, whereas the Pharisees represented the current nation and viewed oral law as valid as well. The Pharisees could change, the Sadducees could not.

The Pharisees grew up in the tradition of the synagogue, while the Sadducees developed in the Temple at Jerusalem. Because the Pharisees developed and advocated the synagogues they became the champions or advocates of the common person who could not go to the Temple daily; the Sadducees advocated for the Temple politics and power and became more and more in tune with the political establishment.

Unlike the Samaritans, who developed outside the rest of Jewry, other sectarian groups developed within Judaism with the hope of converting mainstream Judaism to their view. Many of the different views developed more along social and economic lines rather than religious. While the Pharisees and Sadducees fought for political control under the Maccabean and Herod, their differences were not confined to politics. The Sadducees represented the aristocracy and priestly class and were therefore conservative. The Pharisees, as their name suggests were separatists who distanced themselves from the Temple power of the Sadducees. The Pharisees organized themselves into fraternities and imposed a rigid observance of the law. Although their numbers are not known, the Pharisees seemed to enjoy great popularity and represented the views of a large majority of the population.

The Pharisees, unlike the more state-conscious Sadducees, promoted and enjoyed expansion among Jewry outside of Palestine. They successfully proselytized Babylonia, and Hellenized Jewry attracting a wide flowing. Some famous individuals included, for example, Philo in Alexandria, Paul's father in Tarsus, and Paul himself. The Roman Celsus knew only of Jews who believed in the resurrection, that is, Pharisees.

In religion this difference between the two sects carried over as well, because the Sadducees in essence could not believe in change, and thus could not accept such ideas as the resurrection. The Pharisees, on the other hand, being open to new influence, could argue for the soul's being immortal and that the virtuous would live again. Josephus attempted to explain for his Greek audience the ideas of immortality of the soul and the resurrection of the body and pointed out that this resurrection was only for the virtuous.

The Sadducees, geared more for the now, rejected this idea. They furthermore could not find any mention of the resurrection in the Law of Moses. The Sadducees, however, could not stop the movement for good reason—it was popular. If a person's life is truly miserable here on earth, there must be something else giving a sense of hope. Pharisees filled this hope with the belief in immortality of the soul and bodily resurrection.

Another theological difference between the Sadducees and Pharisees concerned the concept of free will and its opposite, predestination. Hellenism impacted the Sadducees in their belief in individualism and that one's actions were solely their own. The Sadducees, according to Josephus, removed fate and therefore God from actions, meaning humans have free choice or free will to do good or evil (*Wars of the Jews* 8.14.164–165). This was in opposition to the Pharisees, who believed in the older tradition of national or universal responsibility. Although not going as far as the Essenes, who believed in complete predestination or fatalism, the Pharisees ended up in the middle. Although stressing individual responsibility, the Pharisees also believed in other influences, such as demons and angels. The Pharisees tapped into elements of popular discontent in which magic, astrology, and popular superstition mingled. Angels, which the Sadducees argued were only messengers, are one example of a force that the Pharisees said influenced humanity. They and their opposites, demons, could tempt a person. The Pharisees would even use rituals reminiscent of pagan mysticism, prompting the Sadducees to mock them. The popular ideas of demons and their forces are seen in several passages of the New Testament in which Jesus and later his disciples drive them out of individuals and thus curing them. For example, Jesus drives a slew of demons, named Legion, out of a man into a flock of pigs, which then commit suicide.

Perhaps one of the interesting differences between the Sadducees and Pharisees concerned their religious institution of worship. As the traditional priestly class aligned closely with the physical political state, the Sadducees were tied closely with the Temple and its practices. They derived their power and wealth from the Temple institution and its associated worship. For the individual living in Jerusalem the Sadducees were personification of the Temple. Even for Jews in Judea who traveled to Jerusalem for the annual Jewish feasts days, the Temple was crucial. For example, Luke mentions that Jesus went to Jerusalem with his parents and when not discovered with them they searched, only to find him in the Temple teaching the elders (Luke 2:41–51). The story relates the importance of going to Jerusalem and the Temple. The Pharisees, who never denied the importance and supremacy of the Temple, nevertheless stressed the synagogue. With the Pharisees' philosophy of a universal state, one not confined to Judea, and therefore representing the vast elements of the Diaspora, the synagogue was crucial. It would be through this structure and institution throughout the Mediterranean that Judaism, and therefore the Pharisees and their successors, the rabbis, would preserve Judaism after the destruction of the Temple and the Jewish defeats in 70 and 136 C.E.

The Sadducees and Pharisees differed both religiously and socially. The Pharisees believed not only in the written tradition of the Pentateuch but in the oral tradition handed down after Moses. The Sadducees, however, held the view that the only authority was the written law. Differing on this issue, the Pharisees argued for a continual reinterpretation of the law. It is often viewed, especially in light of the New Testament criticism, that the Pharisees were only interested in applying minutia to the law to make religious life a hindrance. For example, the law prohibits the carrying of food outside the house on the Sabbath. To modern readers this seems nonsense. Are we to believe that the Pharisees did not believe in socializing on the Sabbath? Of course not. What the interpretation really meant was to define the position of the house and therefore to allow the act. In Palestine, especially in cities, the Jewish house was centered on a courtyard with other houses. The interpretation of the ban meant that individuals were not to go outside of the house block; they could go into the courtyard and meet other family members.

The theological differences come out in the New Testament with Jesus constantly arguing for a reinterpretation of the law, even beyond those of the Pharisees. For example, when the Pharisees criticized Jesus' followers for working on the Sabbath, he pointed out that the law was made for man and not the other way around. Jesus of course epitomized the resurrection of the body. The story is the very central idea of Jesus and his message. The New Testament also stressed the importance of angels, first in the archangel Gabriel who arrived and proclaimed Jesus' birth to Mary (Luke 1:26–36). An angel then arrived and told Joseph to marry Mary (Matt. 1:20), an angel announced Jesus' birth (Luke 2:13–15), and finally an angel told Joseph to go to Egypt and return (Matt. 2:13). In these examples Jesus and his followers clearly associated his views with the Pharisees. This pointed out in many ways that Jesus and his followers were steeped in the tradition of the Pharisees.

Zealots

Other groups existed that had different political and religious views about Judaism than mainstream society. The Zealots were one such group, and they argued for violence. Although perhaps a sectarian group, they were more interested in nationalism. The Zealots believed in using violence to rid Palestine of the foreign occupation by Rome. Drawn from a rich history of religion, politics, and military power, the Zealots harkened back to the Maccabees and their victory over the Syrians. Because this victory only occurred through violence, the Zealots believed that only through violence could they throw the Romans out. Although ultimately defeated, they impacted everyday life.

During the first century c.e. an extreme group of the Zealots were the *sicarii* or assassins, who killed not only Roman officials and soldiers but Jews who collaborated with them. Named for the short Roman dagger *(sica)* they populated the mountains and attacked without warning. They were particularly numerous in Galilee due to the terrain, their recent conversion sparking intense beliefs, and the poor economic conditions of the area fostering their behavior and success. Josephus classified them as a separate sect, and social, economic, and political currents justify this view, but religiously they had no distinct theology. During the Great War they found their allies to be the Idumeans, recent converts like themselves. Ordinary individuals would have known and feared them. If a peasant objected to the Zealots they may have been labeled a collaborator and faced retaliation. If they were sympathetic and gave aid and comfort, the Roman authorities would have punished them. In most cases the Zealots and their actions would have incurred a harsh response from Rome. The response in all cases would have hurt the normal individual.

The Zealots, however, were seen as heroes by these same individuals. They were striking a blow against Roman oppression and this in turn gave hope and pride to everyone. The ultimate power was their ability to strike fear, not only in the Roman camps, but in Jewish lives as well.

In the New Testament Jesus is said to have had one Zealot as a follower, and it may be that he thought the hoped-for Messiah would strike at Rome (Luke 6:15). This of course did not happen, and it is probable that most Zealots did not flock to his message. The war against Rome fueled the idea of military Messiah who would lead the Jews to victory. The Zealots proclaimed that the war would produce a victory for them over Rome. With the defeat in the Bar Kochba War and the ultimate disintegration of Judea, the Zealots sank into oblivion.

The Zealots probably followed the theological ideas of the Pharisees. Unlike the Sadducees who tended to keep the peace with Rome, the Zealots believed in armed aggression against Rome.

Essenes

Another group was the Essenes. Josephus mentions them as being in all of the cities. But most of our views and information about them come from the Dead Sea Scrolls and the archaeological material at Qumran. Here a community was established in the second century B.C.E. by a group that viewed the Sadducees and the Temple hierarchy as corrupt. The High Priest John Hyrcanus was portrayed in their writings as evil. What comes out from the material is a vision of complexity. The Essenes were fatalists, believing that all things were predetermined by God. They desired to turn back the clock to a time when life was simpler. They rejected pleasure and did not believe in accommodation like the Sadducees. They seem to have hated women, breaking down into two groups. One group was against all kinds of marriage, while the second, although their community was mainly male, did have some women, but only for procreation.

The sect appears to have been communistic, that is, all goods were held and used by the community. However, some of the texts mention

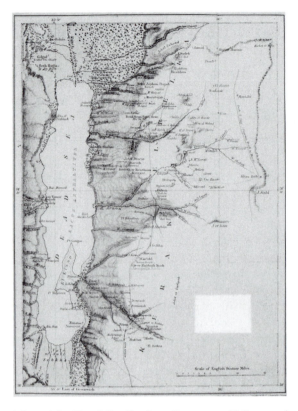

Map of the Dead Sea Region. Courtesy of Library of
Congress.

a penalty to be paid if there was a transgression. This penalty, however,
may refer to those who were initiates and not full members. Finally, there
was a period of time before an individual became a full-fledged member
of the society. The initiate would have a period of time, probably two
years, in which he could explore the ideas of the Essenes but were not
full members and upon final admittance into the sect his goods were then
transferred to the community and they could vote. During this period
of exploration and into the early period of acceptance, the individual
did not have many rights and was expected to defer to the senior members. There was probably a group of elders that was in charge, similar to
the Sanhedrin in Jerusalem. They swore an oath of secrecy and most of
our information is only gleaned from interpreting their texts and archaeological information.

When the Jewish rebellion began in 66 C.E. the Essenes hid their texts
in the caves in and around their community at Qumran. This indicates

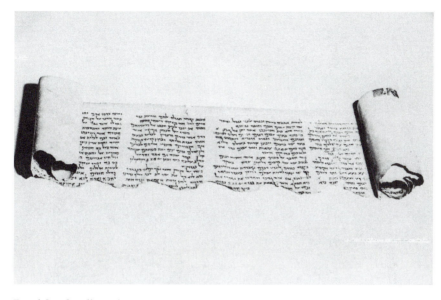

Dead Sea Scrolls and caves and Qumran Excavations of Essene Monastery. Scroll, the Habakkak commentary. Courtesy of Library of Congress.

that they had time to prepare their affairs before fleeing or fighting and that they wished to continue their mission. By hiding the texts they showed that they thought the texts were important and valuable, indicating a desire to see their sect survive. It is impossible to know what ultimately happened, but a few guesses can be made. Because the texts were not recovered by the Essenes, it is probable that the group did not or could not return to Qumran. They may have been wiped out, prevented from coming back, or simply chose not to return. It is probable that they were eliminated, because the evidence does not suggest that at this time Rome prohibited any movement of the population, and it is not clear why they would have just given up their religious ideas and texts. The notion that they became Christians who fled is not supported by any evidence, and most likely they fled either to Jerusalem, where they would have been involved in the siege and probably killed or taken as slaves, or they fled to other cities or into the wilderness. It is possible that their numbers were so depleted in the war that they were unable to reach a critical mass to continue.

This community is fascinating because it gives a glimpse of how one group separated itself from society and how it viewed mainstream Judaism. Their life and community should not be seen as typical. It is possible, although no real evidence exists other than similarities in their ideas, that John the Baptist and Jesus knew of the community.

The Dead Sea Region. Courtesy of Library of Congress.

DEAD SEA SCROLLS

On the northwest shore of the Dead Sea the small community of Qumran and the surrounding caves produced significant discoveries during the late 1940s and 1950s. The first of these discoveries was in 1947 when it was announced that in a cave some ancient texts had been discovered. During the next 10 years in 11 caves a total of more than 900 texts and fragments were discovered. Most of the texts, more than 80%, were written in Hebrew. The most important discoveries included scrolls with the Book of Isaiah; a commentary on the Book of Habakkuk; the Copper Scroll, which purports to detail the valuables of the Temple; the Damascus Document; and the Manual of Discipline. Additionally, other scrolls and fragments show that, with the exception of Esther, every book of the Old Testament is represented, and non-Biblical works such as the Manual of Discipline, The Rule of the

Congregation, The Rule of the Blessing, and the War of the Sons of Light Against the Sons of Darkness, are also represented.

The Biblical texts now allow the earliest material from the Hebrew Bible to be dated to before 200 B.C.E. The number and breadth of Biblical material clearly indicate that the community was somehow involved in Jewish life and religion. But who the community was is still debated. While most scholars believe that the Qumran community was associated with the Essenes, that view has not won universal support. Regardless of the religious philosophy of the community, it appears that the group separated itself from mainstream Judaism.

The different non-Biblical scrolls offer competing variants of its origins. For example, the Copper Scroll, which lists an inventory of Temple treasures, is taken to indicate that there was some connection with the Temple and the siege of Jerusalem in 66 C.E. This is possible, but it could also be an artifact of an earlier period that ended up in Qumran after its usefulness had expired. The Damascus Scroll likewise may indicate a connection with another sect, or it may have merely been a copy of a rule that had come into possession of the Qumran community. Because of alternate possibilities modern scholars have continually debated the origins, date, purpose, and philosophy of the community.

The debate about the texts has not been only over their ancient history. Since their discovery, the texts have been the subject of controversy concerning their publication. The original discovery team refused for more than 30 years to release photographs of the unpublished material because they believed that the scrolls were their own personal property. Finally, in the late 1980s, the pace of publication increased because of international pressure. At present, nearly all of the texts have been published and are being digitized.

Just as important as the texts are the archaeological remains found at Qumran. The remains indicate a community of about 150 members. There were several large buildings, one identified as a meeting house. The archaeological remains discovered include textiles, pottery, stone jars, leather goods, and coins. Based on this material, scholars now believe that the Qumran community began during the period of the Maccabees in the second century B.C.E., that there was an earthquake that destroyed a large section of the region and prompted the abandonment of the site, and that in the first century C.E. it was reoccupied until 68 C.E.

The Essenes believed women to be inferior and impure. As such they considered marriages necessary but not worthy. They taught that it was best to keep the sexes separate. The Essenes engaged in ritualistic washings. For the Essenes the importance of the purification was to make the soul and body clean. The Essenes believed that the body was not only impure but corrupt. The body was destined to waste away while the soul would remain. The ritual bathing was to cleanse the soul to make it immortal. Since the Essenes believed the body to be impure they probably did not believe in the resurrection of the body, similar to the Sadducees whom they however thought of as evil. Since resurrection implied that the body would achieve perfection, this was incompatible with Essene ideology. For them the soul was the only thing that mattered.

The Essenes had a structure in which there was an initiation period, probably of two years, in which the initiate learned about the group. During this time the initiate was not a full member. After this probationary period the individual would become a full member and be able to vote and make decisions.

A subgroup or relative of the Essenes were the New Covenanters or Damascus Sect. They, like the Essenes, moved beyond the Pharisees; for example, their rigid interpretation of the laws made them more akin to the Sadducees. Like the Essenes and probably Pharisees, they required an oath from initiates. They repudiated the Temple and annual sacrifices, probably due to the image of the corruption in Jerusalem by the Sadducees. They had a philosophy of war, seen in their image of the Children of Light versus the Children of Dark, which they equated with the Temple and Jerusalem. Both of these sects removed themselves from society and desired to return to some golden age of Judaism where life was simpler. Unlike the Sadducees, who merely attempted to not deal with the change in society, and the Pharisees, who attempted to change as society changed, the Essenes and similar groups attempted to actively resist the changes by separating themselves from society. Their removal from society really meant that they had little impact upon the development of Judaism. With their secrecy, outsiders like Josephus could only guess as to what they believed. Their texts, often allegorical, require much interpretation, and the archaeological remains are inconclusive. Although these groups may not have greatly impacted the daily lives of many in the New Testament period, they nevertheless show that other groups existed and were constantly a factor in society. In many ways they are akin in scope to religious separatists who establish communities on the fringes of modern society; they are not highly influential, but they are recognized.

The first century B.C.E. to the century C.E. produced a variety of philosophies in Judaism, each competing with one another. At the end of the first century C.E. only two philosophies really remained, the Pharisees through the synagogues, and another offshoot, Christianity. These two philosophies dominated the daily life in the New Testament.

Scribes

A group often associated with the Pharisees was the Scribes. Were they a separate sect or part of the Pharisees? This is not really clear; they started in the time of Ezra, and they were the scholars who interpreted the law. In the Gospels they were called "lawyers" and "teachers of the Law"; they were really the scholars of Judaism (Luke 5:17, 7:30). They attempted to explain the points of the law and give opinions about how one should live the law. In many ways they gave force of teaching to the Pharisees and their interpretation of the law. Since Galilee at the time of Jesus was backward, without educated and trained religious teachers, its people were more fanatical and unlearned; the Scribes were seen more in Judea. They may not have been a subgroup of the Pharisees, but they probably had more in common with them than with the Sadducees. The scribes and Pharisees were seen as sticklers for the law.

Since most of the gospels were written after the destruction of Jerusalem, the Sadducees, Zealots, Essenes, and other groups are not seen in the New Testament. While the Sadducees might be mentioned, they were usually not well-defined or separated from the Pharisees, with the major exception of the differences in belief in resurrection. With the Temple gone and Judea completely ravaged, the only remaining component of Judaism was embodied in the Pharisees. Judaism that existed outside of Palestine now became the dominant form, and since this group was mainly from the Pharisees, it is that group that survived. With this survival what also survived was their view of what the Messiah would be. They now viewed that the Messiah was promised but would not necessarily come soon. With the destruction of the Temple, the image of a political/military Messiah ended. Within this context Christianity now separated itself from Judaism.

The view that Jesus was the Messiah now provided the split between the sects in Palestine. The split produced not only different philosophies but practices. In addition to Jesus being the Messiah who rose from the dead, Christians also further developed the ideas of heaven and hell that had already begun under Judaism but were not fully developed. The major differences in this early period centered on the practices.

One of the first major changes was the place of worship. Unlike Jews who worshipped in synagogues, the early Christians now began to worship in their own structures. The first such structures were the house churches. Originally private residences, the house churches ultimately became public spaces to worship. Unlike the synagogue, which had preset designs and which faced Jerusalem, the house churches took on no particular design and instead were modeled on the room of the Last Supper, a large gathering room. Later the Christians developed their own type of structure, the basilica, borrowed from the Roman civic building.

Unlike the Jewish days of celebration, Mondays and Thursdays, the early Christians set aside Wednesdays and Fridays. Both were days for fasting and meetings, the *synaxis,* with the Eucharist celebrated. Both days celebrated days of Christ's suffering, Wednesday the day Judas betrayed Jesus, and Friday the day Jesus died. They were mentioned as special days in the late first-century manual of worship, the Didache, and the works of second-century writers such as Hermas and Tertullian. Sunday, the day

Christ rose from the dead, became the most important day of the week, replacing the Jewish Sabbath on Saturday. Using this day as the central weekly religious celebration made the cleavage between Judaism and Christianity complete. Saturday still retained some importance in Rome as a day of fasting and penance in preparation for Sunday's importance.

These early meetings centered on the traditional Jewish services but now became formalized using Christian beliefs. The early Christians had two important ceremonies, baptism/confirmation and the Eucharist, which separated Christians from mainstream Jews. Baptism, representing the crossing over from dying, not believing, and living, believing, meant to wash and cleanse an initiate of their sins and release demons from their souls. This idea seems to have been borrowed from the Essenes, which believed in baptism and had an elaborate ceremony. Baptism in which individuals were immersed in water and a seal in oil was made on the forehead was reserved for adults. For the Christians the period before Easter, Lent, was for the initiate's preparation, with baptism occurring on Holy Saturday. Judaism did not have this period before the Paschal celebration. Once the initiate was baptized, they received confirmation, the imposition of hands and the use of oil on their foreheads, although some had their whole body rubbed with oil. The chrism, oil mixed with balsam, became the symbol for confirmation, like water was for baptism. In the early Church, confirmation was called the "imposition of hands" or "of the hand." The ceremony took place on Holy Saturday after baptism. With the completion of these two sacraments, the final ceremony, the Eucharist, was then celebrated. The Eucharist celebrated the final difference between the Christians and Jews, for here Christ was now represented in worldly form, bread and wine.

JEW VERSUS GENTILE

The distinction between early Christianity and Judaism was not clear or precise, because both Jews and gentiles composed the early Church, both claiming preeminence. The initial debate that led to a distancing of the groups arose over circumcision. Previously, a male gentile converting to Judaism underwent circumcision, a painful act for adults, which signified the individual's acceptance of the covenant between God and his chosen people, the Jews. Many gentiles, however, heard the early Christian missionaries, especially Peter and Paul, and desired to become members of this Church. This desire to follow Christ led to a discussion on whether an individual had to first become a Jew and then a Christian, necessitating circumcision. At the council of Antioch Peter argued and prevailed against such a necessity, and gentiles no longer had to convert to Judaism before becoming Christian. This decision, not accepted by all the early followers, created a division in early Christianity between Jewish Christians and gentile Christians. The Jewish Christians, represented by

James, one of the original 12, and leader of the Jewish Christians in Jerusalem, sought to have Christianity fulfill the ideas of the Old Testament and the concept of the Messiah for the Jews. In his view Christianity was for the Jews and fulfilled the ancient promise of a Messiah. Individuals who believed in Jesus as the Messiah therefore had to become Jewish.

This division between Jewish and Gentile Christians is best seen in the early Christian manual, the Didache, which discussed, among other things, the issue of dietary laws, fasting, and worship days. Although probably written by a Jewish Christian, the manual was clearly intended for the gentile convert. Gentiles no longer followed the strict Jewish dietary laws; whereas Jews, and presumably Jewish Christians, fasted on Mondays and Thursdays, the gentile Christians were encouraged to fast on Wednesdays and Fridays. Finally, Jews and Jewish Christians kept the Sabbath day (Saturday) holy, while the gentile Christians kept Sunday holy, in commemoration of Christ's resurrection. These differences produced changes in the daily life of Christians. Whereas Jewish Christians would continue to be seen as a subsect of Judaism, these changes in dietary laws, fasting, and worship days placed the gentile Christians outside mainstream Jewish life and more into Greco-Roman life, where they could blend into Roman society. This assimilation, however, was not complete, for unlike pagan inhabitants, Christians refused to celebrate the pagan festivals, which often drew attention to them and may have led to persecutions.

The change that occurred in Palestine with the separation of the Jewish followers of Jesus had a profound influence on daily life. No longer were individuals who followed Christ tied to the ancient Jewish customs, especially concerning circumcision and dietary rules. In addition, with the change from synagogues to house churches, the need for followers to adhere to specific Jewish buildings was also removed. Finally, with the split, the Temple no longer was all-important. All of these changes influenced the daily life of believers in Jesus not only in Palestine, but in the rest of the Roman world.

6

TRADES AND PROFESSIONS

And you yourselves be like men who wait for their master, when he will return from the wedding, that when he comes and knocks they may open to him immediately. Blessed are those servants whom the master, when he comes, will find watching. Assuredly, I say to you that he will gird himself and have them sit down to eat, and will come and serve them. And if he should come in the second watch or come in the third watch, and find them so, blessed are those servants. But know this, that if the master of the house had known what hour the thief would come, he would have watched and not allowed his house to be broken into. (Luke 12:36–39)

In the New Testament there are a variety of occupations mentioned that were probably typical of the time. This chapter will explore the various occupations and the influence they had on society. One's occupation placed the individual in society. During the course of time different occupations were seen as belonging to the upper class, middle class, or lower class, which could change from time to time.

BUILDERS

To begin, Jesus' father Joseph was a carpenter. This was a professional trade and was probably a middle-class profession. A carpenter made household furnishings, tables, chairs, chests, and other goods. Because this required skill, a carpenter should be seen as a skilled workman requiring training, rather than a laborer. This training normally required several years as an apprentice. Upon completing his training, a carpenter could ply his trade and become a respected member of a community. This position gave him access to power, and his family would have received education, respect, and local political power. For example, Jesus, the son of a carpenter, obviously learned how to read because in the Gospels it is mentioned that he read in the local synagogue and then preached. His father's social position would have made Jesus acceptable to the local community in terms of reading and preaching in the local synagogue. Usually the individual learned his trade from a relative, usually his father. Although there is no evidence that Jesus practiced as a carpenter, he is mentioned as a carpenter's son, and it may be reasonable to assume that he learned his father's trade.

Another trade similar to carpentry was stone mason or builder. Although not directly mentioned in the Gospels, there is reference to them when Jesus' followers mention how beautifully the Temple was adorned (Mark 13:1–2; Luke 21:5). Stonemasons, especially during Herod the Great's reign, were in great demand for finishing the Temple and building the city of Caesarea, especially the port. The stonemasons were needed to ensure the structures were built soundly and that the facades, often adorned with marble, were pleasing. In addition to general stonemasons, those who worked in marble, specialized stonemasons, were given even more importance. They had to know how to attach the surfaces to the stone and polish them. Recently archaeologists have discovered a quarry in Jerusalem where evidence appears that it was used during Herod's reign. The excavations point to a large quarry where stone blocks weighing as much as 20 tons were cut and used in a large project. Although it is impossible to know for sure if the Temple was that project, the evidence indicates that it was used during Herod's reign and for a great project, one for which the Temple qualifies.

LEATHER AND CLOTHING WORKERS

The New Testament mentions those who work in leather and its ancillary trades, tent makers and tanners. Paul of Tarsus had training in these trades. Leather workers were extremely important because they made clothes, bags, horse gear, and other accoutrements. Again, this trade required training and experience. Leather workers were in demand by merchants, the public, and the military. The amount of leather goods required was immense. For example, an everyday individual might need shoes, a small purse or bag, wine or water sacks, a larger bag for carrying goods, and if they were engaged in trade they might need covers to put over a cart or sacks for products. The making of tents was required by the military for maneuvers and campaigns. In the East this need would have been substantial, because the army in Syria comprised at least three legions. Because the army had a constant turnover in troops it required a steady supply of shoes, leather armor, shields that required leather straps, horse accoutrements, and other goods. Merchants required tents because they traveled from town to town, often in unsettled areas, and would require temporary housing. They would also need leather goods for camel and horse supplies, materials for carrying and storing goods, and wagon implements such as straps and covers. Again with the need for goods being carried throughout the eastern Mediterranean, leather materials were constantly in demand.

Those who worked in cloth were also in high demand. While most of the clothes were made in the home, some shops produced clothing for the upper classes. These shops also produced coarser clothes for common people. A typical shop would have had a master weaver who would have owned or managed the shop. If the master weaver only managed the shop the owner may have been a wealthy individual who owned land or shops or worked in other income-producing trades. The master weaver may not have even performed the work, having others who did the actual work. The shop may have had numerous workers at different ranks doing the weaving. After the master weaver there would have been those who had proven themselves as producers of high-quality works that sold well. Below them would have been those who were capable and produced material acceptable to the masses.

Finally at the bottom was the apprentice. The contract for the apprentice usually had several components. First there was the time period in which the apprentice agreed to serve. The time was usually one year, although there were times when it could be more or less, six months to three years. This time period usually indicated how many days a month the apprentice would work, and how many hours a day. The contract would indicate what the master would provide in terms of keep and wages. There was usually a requirement for payment of taxes, usually paid by the master. Finally, some contracts required the apprentice to work for the master after the term of apprenticeship was over.

There were a variety of different clothing materials that one could use, depending on one's economic means. At the upper end was silk, which was imported from China. These goods could be worked into fine undergarments as well as colorful outerwear. Silk-workers were well paid and predominately employed by the wealthy and powerful. Linen was also highly prized. The most common material was wool. An ancillary profession to weavers, but more profitable, were those who dyed the yarn for wool and silk that were then used by the weavers. Although not mentioned exactly, there is a mention of dealer in purple fabrics in the Acts of the Apostles (Acts 16:14), indicating that there were dyers involved. This is confirmed from nonbiblical sources that indicate that in Tyre there was a booming business in dyed fabrics.

FISHING

Another trade directly mentioned in the New Testament was fishing. For example several of Jesus' followers were fishermen (Mark 1:16–20). Again, the trade was professional because fishermen had to make and mend nets, navigate and sail, and act as merchants. They were not just simple peasants who rowed out and dropped a pole. Fishermen had to have professional training in matters relating to sailing and at the same time they had to be merchants who could sell their catch. The region of Galilee around the Sea of Tiberius (the Lake of Galilee) is mentioned in the New Testament. Jesus called several fishermen to be his followers. The Gospels also mention that Jesus and his followers went by boat to regions across the Lake of Tiberius or were out on the lake where Jesus is said to have come out during a storm or where Jesus was sleeping and then awoke during a storm and calmed the sea (Matt. 8:23–27). The importance of these stories here is that the profession of the seafarer was important and crucial to the region.

TAX COLLECTORS

Professions that were looked down upon but were nevertheless important and mentioned in the New Testament were the accountants, tax collectors, or custom house officials (Luke 5:27–32). Seen as individuals who were ready to seize a neighbor's house or property in the name of Rome, the tax collector was not only despised but seen as a traitor or collaborator. They needed to have knowledge of writing, reading, and accounting as well as the ability to deal with individuals, both government officials and the general public. Because they often were from the local population, they had to walk a fine line between abusing their own people and yet placating the government. These individuals were called the *publicani* and were seen by their own people as traitors. They had to know how to prevent being abused (or at least not too much) by the government officials who wanted to enrich themselves, and how to read and negotiate with people who did not want to pay their taxes and who would come up with numerous excuses and stories.

An ancillary of these trades would be those in banking. In the ancient world banking was often associated with the pagan temples. These temples acted as safety deposit boxes that allowed people to ensure their possessions. There also existed banks, which made loans to merchants, landowners, and others. An example of a banker was the Roman general and politician Marcus Licinius Crassus, a colleague of Julius Caesar who made some of his money by lending sums to wealthy Roman landowners who were cash-strapped. By charging interest, often above the standard Roman practice of 12 percent, Crassus enriched himself. These bankers existed throughout the Mediterranean world and continually made loans and collected interest from all classes. The laws against usury were usually bypassed if the person who made the loan was not a Roman. Of course there were risks involved for the lender. If the borrower was a Roman it was sometimes hard to collect if there was not an airtight contract, because the Romans could argue that they were exempt from such contracts. In Judaism there were strict legal regulations concerning borrowing and lending. Documents paid by the debtor were written out in front of witnesses and signed, ensuring that one could not dispute its authenticity. The sum borrowed was not only indicated at the top of the document but inside the body as well. Interest seems to have been less than the Roman rate of 1 percent per month or 12 percent per year. One could take a pledge but only under certain conditions; for example, one could not take pledges from a widow. Whereas Roman practice was based upon the law, Jewish practice attempted to ensure that religious practice was followed.

Associated with banking would be the money changers. Throughout the Mediterranean during this time were local currencies, which were used in the local markets. While Roman coins were used throughout the empire, local bronze coins could be used as well. Cities would issue their own coins and usually required that foreign coins be exchanged. This exchange of course produced a profit for the money changers. They would take a percentage or not give the full market value, similar to what occurs today when tourists travel abroad and attempt to change their currency into the local money. In Palestine money changers played an important role because it was required that the Temple tax be paid with Jewish coins. Jewish coinage had to be used for the purchasing of sacrifices used in the Temple. In addition merchants are mentioned in the Temple who dealt in cattle, sheep, and pigeons, the actual sacrifices (Matt. 21:13–17; Mark 11:15–19).

In addition to tax collectors, who were seen as despicable, another role mentioned in the same light were prostitutes, often referred to as sinners. Most societies have women and men who engage in this practice, often due to economic circumstances. Ancient society often tried to regulate and discourage the practice, but it is clear in the New Testament that Roman and Jewish officials did not outlaw prostitution. Papyri from Egypt occasionally record the collection of prostitute taxes. Some scholars have argued that the term *sinner* mentioned in the Gospels, especially concerning Mary Magdalene, might not have referred to prostitution, but rather may have been an attack on her to diminish her standing in the early Church. She may in fact have simply been a follower of Jesus. But prostitution was a profession that permeated society. There were several layers that existed in society. At the lowest level was the independent prostitute, who had the least amount of protection and was often the one most at risk. There were the prostitutes who had pimps who attempted to procure clients and protect the workers. They had a bit more security, but more depended upon their ability to navigate the social classes of their clients. At the next level were the brothels, which had numerous workers, both women and men, and had more protection. These houses not only employed their own guards but may have had some official protection from the local police and government, for a price of course. At the highest level were the workers who serviced the aristocracy. They usually had enough connections to ensure their position and protection. It appears that the prostitutes mentioned in the Gospels came from the lower levels of society.

The Gospels mention merchants in general terms, probably referring to the normal traders who moved throughout the Mediterranean world. They might engage in long-distance trade, using the excellent port built by Herod the Great at Caesarea; regional trade between Egypt, Arabia, or Syria using camels; or local trade within the provinces and surrounding area using mules and wagons. These merchants provided access to a variety of goods and allowed Palestinian goods to be sent abroad. Many of them would have had ties in Palestine, especially with powerful and rich Jewish landowners. These merchants, especially those dealing in long-distance trade, had offices in other cities such as Alexandria and Ostia, Rome's port. Because there was a sizeable contingent of Jewish inhabitants in Alexandria and Rome, it is reasonable to assume that some were engaged as agents for Palestinian merchants.

AGRICULTURE

The Gospels mention the major occupation of the time, agriculture, which included a variety of occupations. The Gospel of Luke mentions shepherds associated with Jesus' birth (Luke 1:14). The countryside could support sheep in great numbers, which were thus an important commodity. In addition to wool, the major product, sheep were also used for food and in religious sacrifices. Wool was the most important commodity, however, because it was crucial for clothing. Not mentioned in the New Testament, but seen in other texts, there were workers who spun the wool, worked the looms, and produced garments. Because wool is excellent for both summer and winter clothing, it was in great demand. Those who worked wool are also mentioned in other documents. In addition to shearing the sheep of their wool, workers were needed to spin the wool into yarn. There was a need to then weave the yarn into garments. At each stage there was a level of complexity needed. For example, the weaver was considered a tradesman, while those who sheared the sheep were not.

Another agricultural occupation was viticulture. The New Testament makes several references to working in the vineyards (Matt. 20:1–16; Mark 12:1–11). Wine was an important commodity in the ancient world. Although water was the main drink, wine closely followed. The story of the wedding feast at Cana clearly shows that wine was used in celebratory meals. The references of the Last Supper indicate that in religious services such as the Seder, wine was commonly employed. The Mediterranean region with its mild winters was well-suited for the growing of grapes.

Vineyards and olive groves near Bethlehem.
Courtesy of Library of Congress.

In many areas grapes became the most important commercial crop, being made into wine and transported throughout the Roman Empire. Coupled with vineyards were those who engaged in the cultivation of olives and the production of olive oil. Olive oil was used for a variety of needs, such as for supplying lamps with fuel, cooking, bathing as soap, and preserving other agricultural goods. The cultivation required a heavy commitment of capital and time, especially because it took years for a tree to mature and bear fruit.

The most important occupation in agriculture was wheat farming. Wheat was used for the making of bread, the major sustenance in society. The New Testament mentions the parable of the farmer sowing wheat on different terrains (Luke 8:5–8). For the listener or reader of this story it must have been all too familiar. The importance of the farmer, together with the miller who ground the wheat, and the baker who made the bread, cannot be underestimated. Although the New Testament may not give explicit examples of all these trades, they must have been important because there was a significant population, in Jerusalem and the other cities, who were not engaged in agriculture and who needed bread. The local inhabitants must have relied on a large number of agricultural workers, both on the farm and in the city, to supply them with their food. A local community would have been supplied with the grain from the surrounding farms, which would have been transported into the cities or villages by local transporters.

Although the New Testament does not give explicit examples of how this worked, papyri from Egypt help in our understanding. The records from Egypt clearly indicate that the communities were supplied with local grain, carried in sacks from the farms to local receiving points, often mills. The grain was then made into flour and then sold to local bakeries. The sources indicate that some farmers, especially those who were wealthy or powerful, had mills on their own property, thus making their employees more reliant on the owners. The evidence shows that most of the local markets were supplied with local goods. Abuses, however, did arise. Some individuals clearly increased their power due to their ability to control the livelihood of the local community members. Large estates flourished and these landowners often abused their position. There are complaints in the Talmud of some wealthy individuals buying water rights to force smaller farm owners to sell. In addition to farmers there are references to farm laborers, that is, those who did not own a farm but worked on one. These laborers fell into several classes: slaves, tenants, and casual or day laborers. The agricultural situation in the New Testament was very complex, with people moving in and out of their respective duties and occupations. For example, a farmer might also be a transporter some of the time and might then be a merchant. The size of the farm also had an impact. Small farms tended to be worked by families in which all members did multiple jobs, while large estates tended to have specializations. The economy needed both the large and small farms because they provided services to different groups in society.

THE TEMPLE ECONOMY

Another occupation had to deal with the sacrifices in the Temple. The workings of the Temple sacrifice required individuals to procure animals, and they had to know the intricacies of legal requirements for pure and clean animals. Workers were also needed to ensure that the animals were kept alive and cared for until their sacrifice, and others were needed to clean the Temple and care for the removal of remains. Workers were required to supply wood for the fires. Merchants would also supply incense and other materials needed for Temple sacrifices. The Temple employed its own security, the Temple guards, who not only ensured protection but also enforced the distinctions of who could enter the different precepts (Matt. 26:51–52; Luke 22:52; John 18:12).

Merchants were an integral part of the Temple, supplying not only the sacrificial animals, such as doves or lambs, but also services for travelers. For example, visitors from outside of Palestine had to convert their currency, such as Roman or Greek coins, into Jewish coins for the contribution to the Temple. These money changers, mentioned in the New Testament, of course charged for their services. The image of Jesus overturning the money changers' tables provides a vivid picture of the differences between the urban Temple complex and the rural visitors (Luke 19:45–46).

NONBIBLICAL

The occupations mentioned in the New Testament were not the only ones in existence. There are numerous other trades and professions. For example, one of the lowest classes of work, usually reserved for criminals, was mining. Mention is made in other documents of mines in Palestine where the condemned were forced to carry out their sentences, often until death. Another trade was quarrying, cutting the stones and transporting them to cities, ports, and military regions.

Goatherders were in the same category as shepherds. They were not tradesmen but rather isolated individuals who tended the flocks that supplied the region with wool and other goods. Camel and muleteers were needed to carry goods throughout the region. Camels were especially useful because the desert climate was too harsh on horses and mules. In the coastal regions mules were used for transport. The Mishnah has a rabbi saying that a man should not educate his son to be a donkey-driver, camel-driver, barber, sailor, shepherd, or peddler, because those who held these occupations were like thieves. But another rabbi indicated that although donkey-drivers were wicked, camel-drivers were honest and sailors pious.

There were specialized trades that were in the same category as carpenters. One such group of tradesman would be the smiths. At the top were the goldsmiths. This trade required not only wealth, because they would have to have gold on hand, but also great skill because gold was very difficult to work with. There would not be many goldsmiths, because not only was gold expensive but the number of individuals who could purchase these goods were confined to a very few. Silver, cheaper and sturdier than gold, was next and more common because middle-class people could afford to purchase silver goods (Acts 19:23 mentions a silver smith who made statues). These two kinds of smithing were done for and from the upper class. Coppersmiths were also important because copper was used for cooking instruments. Because most middle-class households could afford copper cooking implements, they were in more use and demand. Iron- or blacksmiths were again of a specialized nature because these metals were used for military and farm implements.

These smiths were supplemented by other workers such as potters. Potters also were of varying class and expertise. At the bottom were the common potters who created the everyday jugs and plates for use in nearly every house. These goods were cheaply made using the local clay and fire kilns. At a higher level were the potters who created goods for the middle class and public taverns and inns. These were sturdier and finer quality. The jugs, bowls, and plates could withstand repeated use. At the top were the finest qualities of plate made not only of finer qualities but richly ornate. A specialized form of potters would have been the makers of amphora, which allowed for the transport of goods across great distances. These amphoras of varying sizes and shapes allowed wine, oil, grain, and other goods to be carried by camel, mule, and ships. Often they were re-used at the point of destination to allow for return cargo and occasionally were used in ships for ballast when filled with sand.

Sailmaking was also an important trade in Palestine and throughout the Near East during the first century. The need for these sailmakers can be seen in association with the journey of Paul. Paul, traveling on a large sea-going vessel, was being transported to Italy when shipwrecked. The seagoing vessels were important for long-distance trade, making trade cheaper and allowing for more quantity to be transported from one region to the other. Associated with the sailmakers were the other tradesmen and workers who constructed ships. In addition to carpenters, there was a need for ropemakers and shipwrights who had specialized knowledge of shipbuilding.

Another often-overlooked individual was the cook. Again, there were different classes, from the family cook to the palace cook. A good cook was always an important necessity to an aristocratic family. Associated with the cook would be the steward, one in charge of wine stock and in general in charge of the household. These servants, together with the butler, en-sured that the house functioned smoothly. A porter, mentioned in the New Testament, was not only one who announced the arrival of guests but en-sured that the house was protected and a maid is mentioned in Luke who accuses Peter of being a follower of Jesus (Luke 22:56).

There were also a host of local shopkeepers who were needed to en-sure the functioning of a city. For example, there were the numerous food shops, which provided not only the local inhabitants but visitors with op-portunities to obtain food and drink. In the ancient cities this was impor-tant, because many of the households could not have fires for cooking due to fire hazards. Tavern- or inn-owners not only served food but drink, which was also important. The taverns were social areas as wells. Indi-viduals not only used taverns for food and drink but as hotels and sources of entertainment. Like hotels, they provided important amenities for visi-tors. The level of comfort depended upon the type of guest. Guests were given a variety of options. For example, a wealthy patron could have a series of rooms or suites. In addition they could have better meals and even have access to the baths. Depending upon the tavern, there would be accessibility to entertainment: dancing, drinking, gambling, and sex. These taverns were located throughout all the cities and on the roadways. An example in the New Testament of such a place concerned the parable of the Good Samaritan, who finds a traveler who had been beaten on the road and takes him to an inn (Luke 10:23–37).

In Acts, Paul worked as a tentmaker and probably was a leather worker. It is apparent that he was able to practice this trade not only in his home city of Antioch but in other cities in the Greek world (Acts 10:32). This provides us with an interesting concept, the notion that people could in fact practice their trades, probably with help from someone who was willing to accept their work, throughout the Roman world. In Paul's case it was probably due to a fellow Christian who accepted his aid or allowed him to work as a way to ensure his ability to carrying out his missionary activities.

Rabbis during the time of Jesus also engaged in a variety of trades that they considered honorable. Some engaged in woodworking, carpentry, and building, while others were tailors, smiths, shoemakers, or potters. In other words, these rabbis believed that manual labor was honorable and nothing to be ashamed of. The rabbis also clearly valued work and argued that people should be able to provide support for their families.

Jewish sources indicate that some professions were also considered risky if they involved too much interaction between the sexes. These included makers of jewelry, perfumes, and clothing. The goal here of course was to protect the dignity of the woman and her reputation while not threatening the man's position.

The workers considered most important were those who were employed in the Temple, who were necessary for the workings of the Temple and its sacrifices. When the Temple was built the workers were all priests, who had to be specially trained. The Mishnah describes that no iron tools were used in the cutting of the altar stones out of the quarry and that no iron was used in the Temple itself. Those who constructed this great structure did so according to the dictums of their beliefs and ensured that the law was dutifully carried out.

Slavery

Although not a specific trade or occupation, slaves were a vital part of the economy. Slaves could have been engaged in the household or in the field. Household slaves were not confined to merely being house servants. A household slave could work in a shop or small production facility. Weavers might have slaves who worked side by side with apprentices. These slaves tended to be educated or showed some aptitude and willingness to work in these professions. A slave in the house might be a porter, cook, waiter, nanny, driver, or teacher (Mark 14:47). A field slave, on the other hand, had to deal not only with the harsh elements but could work in the mines, quarries, shipyards, or worst yet, be a galley slave. The field slave did not have a good chance to survive and be freed or manumitted as did the house slave.

SOLDIERS

One profession that is not mentioned much in the New Testament is soldiering. Units composed of Jewish soldiers were known to be posted in the Roman army throughout the empire. A hypothetical situation can be reconstructed that may help explain the lure and possibilities. As the Romans needed more and more units to serve on the frontier during the early empire, local units backed up the Roman legionnaires. These local units were auxiliaries. A Jewish peasant, son of a small landowner, who could not possibly inherit his father's farm because he was the youngest of four sons, looks for possible advancements. Upon turning 16 a local recruiter who gets paid signing bonuses for enlisting young men tells the boy of a possible future in the Roman army. One of the opportunities presented to the recruit is the possibility of traveling throughout the empire and seeing the world. This was a traditional selling point for the military.

Another selling point for the recruit would be a steady paycheck. Earning more than he would at home, along with having his necessities provided for, the recruit would have an easier life than his family, especially if there was a famine. The recruit would have had even more possibilities, because soldiers often extorted money from the local population. John the Baptist told soldiers who asked what should they do not to intimidate anyone or accuse falsely, and to be content with their wages (Luke 3:10–14). The implication here is that soldiers were routinely shaking down individuals to increase their pay. When entered in the army the new soldier had opportunities to rise in rank. If the auxiliary survived for 25 years he could retire. One of the benefits would be Roman citizenship not only for himself, but for his children. An example is supposedly Paul, who claimed Roman citizenship, most likely through his father. The retired son could now return home if he wished with his retirement bonus and his new status. With these rewards he could in fact increase his social rank and provide a better life for his family than if he had remained at home.

During the time of the New Testament individuals engaged in work as they had done for hundreds of years. The Romans provided political and military security for the region and in so doing provided economic stability. This economic stability allowed for the common people to be more concerned about their economic livelihoods and less worried about their personal safety. This peace or at least lack of foreign involvement allowed individuals to attempt to advance themselves in society and allowed their children more opportunities. Work opportunities in the first century C.E. provided security, prosperity, and opportunities for advancement.

7

RURAL LIFE AND URBAN LIFE

A sower went out to sow his seed. And as he sowed, some fell by the wayside; and it was trampled down, and the birds of the air devoured it. Some fell on rock; and as soon as it sprang up, it withered away because it lacked moisture. And some fell among thorns, and the thorns sprang up with it and choked it. But others fell on good ground, sprang up, and yielded a crop a hundredfold. (Luke 8:5–8)

RURAL LIFE AND AGRICULTURE

During the first century most of the arable land had already been cleared in Palestine. Any new lands cleared probably corresponded to new regions that originally were deemed as wasteland. With the arrival of peace after Octavian's (Augustus's) victory over Antony and Cleopatra the ancient world at this time witnessed a movement to put more land under cultivation due to the increase in population. This new land came mainly from either wastelands, especially in areas that had already had a history of intensive agriculture, such as Palestine, or from new (wooded/scrub) lands such as Britain or Gaul. Any new land in Palestine would need to be cleared of trees, stumps, and rocks and then would be ready for plowing.

Seasons

For the farmer the time of year dictated daily life. With dry summers and wet winters the climate dictated the cycle. The ground was plowed in the late fall before the rainy season. Using a plow made of wood with a metal blade, pulled by oxen, donkeys, or humans if necessary, the soil was turned, making it ready for planting. The soil was not heavy as in Northern Europe, and in fact a hoe could even be used to plow land. To break up the soil the farmer would first use the hoe or mattock, splitting clumps or "plow" on steep or cramped fields. The plow made of wood and in a curved J shape tipped with iron allowed for the furrows to be made.

Between November and January the seeds were scattered and then covered by a hoe or plow. As Jesus related in the parable, seeds were often eaten by birds, which necessitated careful watching and using scarecrows. To provide more nourishment, compost made of wood ashes, refuse, or animal waste was spread over the soil. It may have been added before or after plowing. Manure was applied to trees and fields. The ashes used were probably from the burning of the stubble in the field rather than burning the plants elsewhere and then spreading them. This type of practice is still often used. The use of the Sabbath or seventh-year fallow allowed the soil to maintain its fertility. Crop rotation was also used. Using a two-field system, one field was planted in the fall while the other lay fallow. Since Palestine had only one growing season for grains, there were only two fields, unlike in Northern Europe where winter crops allowed for the creation of a third field. Using field rotation, only 50 percent of land was used in any given year.

During this time the winter rains provided water. For grains the two main crops sown were barley and wheat. Barley matures before wheat and was harvested in April, and wheat was harvested in May, along with oats. Since oats required more water they were often planted in the bottom lands where water pooled. Oats were not a major grain source. Because Palestine had creeks and streams, irrigation on a massive scale, such as that needed in Egypt, was minimal. Water was raised from wells and could be directed as needed to fields.

Crops, Cooking, and Diet

Crops were often harvested by digging the plants up with the hoe, which allowed the field to be ready for the next planting. But for a large field the grain was cut using a sickle. The harvest began at Passover and ended at Pentecost. The barley harvest coincided with the Festival of Unleavened Bread or Passover (Lev. 23:9–14), while wheat harvest occurred around the Festival of Pentecost about one and a half months later. The book of Exodus calls Pentecost the Feast of Harvest (23:16). It is possible that these two festivals, although ultimately religious, may have started out as rural feasts celebrating the harvest of the two most important foodstuffs. The harvesting of grain, barley, and wheat took nearly two months. The handfuls of wheat were tied into sheaves and then transported to the barns or threshers in baskets or tied into piles and put on donkeys, or if one was wealthy, transported by a wagon.

The sheaves were spread on the floor, which was sometimes nothing more than hardened earth, and animals with or without threshing sledges walked over them, separating the grain from the stalks. The farmer then winnowed the grain by tossing it into the air to allow the lighter chaff to be blown away, while the heavier grain or seed fell to the ground. The grain was then collected and stored. For storing grain farmers could use storage jars for house storage, which provided protection from water, vermin, and the like due the ceramic barrier. Grain was also stored in underground silos, barns, and even caves. For transporting grain the farmer could use sacks or jars (amphorae) loaded on donkeys. Shipments made from the port by sea could use sacks or jars, but jars were often preferred because they provided security and protection from the elements and vermin. The jar was sealed with a hard clay top, which could be used to guarantee that the grain had not been tampered with. Sacks were often employed for times when the grain was to be stored in silos or barns, because men could carry them more easily than jars. The problem with sacks, of course, was that they could be damaged or opened more easily. The average sack weighed about 150 pounds, and three of them could be loaded onto a donkey.

When the grain was shipped, the overseer, whether imperial or commercial, took a sample, supposedly random, and examined the percentage of dirt and other impurities. If the percentage of impurities was too high, for example more than 10 percent, the farmer had to supply extra grain or pay a fine. The overseer would attest to the percentage and give a receipt to both the farmer and shipper. At its destination another sample was taken and compared to the original. If the percentage differed too much the overseer was in trouble. This process ensured that all sides were monitored.

Grain was the main substance grown, and it was used for everyday life. Bread was eaten at every meal and in fact probably accounted for over 70 percent of the caloric value. Flour was made by grinding the wheat or barley using a large stone on the ground, the saddle, and a small upper stone, the rider, pounding the grain into flour. This was then mixed with water and kneaded into dough. The dough was shaped into flat circles and put onto the interior walls of the oven. The oven, which was in the courtyard and heated by wood or charcoal, baked the bread. When done the bread separated from the walls and fell into the ashes below, where it was then brushed clean and used for the meal. The making of bread was therefore a constant exercise.

While vegetables are rarely mentioned in the Bible, and in Proverbs 15:17 are held in low esteem, they must have formed part of the daily diet. Lentils and peas (legumes) were harvested in April and May as well. Their relative unimportance in the sources may reflect the fact that they were harvested at the same time as grain, which was the major source

Ancient stone jar. Courtesy of Library of Congress.

of sustenance. Hence, while not held in high regard in the Bible, this might be due to their harvesting time and that most were grown on small tracts of land near the house. Chickpeas were harvested in June at the beginning of the grape harvest.

Grapes were the most important crop harvested during the summer. Grapes were important not only for food but for wine. The new wine festival occurred 50 days after Pentecost. The grapes were pressed in the vineyards under foot and the juices stored in jars and allowed to ferment. Once fermented the wine was sealed and stored. Wine was served not only at festivals but at nearly every meal and social event. Due to the hilly nature of Palestine, vines were cultivated on the hillsides, which allowed the region to produce a surplus. This surplus was often shipped to other parts of the East, especially Egypt.

Flax, sesame, and millet were also cultivated during the summer, and the other major produce harvested in August and September was figs and pomegranates. By the Feast of Tabernacles the grape harvest was completed.

The last major crop to be harvested was olives, which began in September and lasted until November. Like grapevines, olive trees thrived in the hilly countryside and provided a complement to grain, which grew on the plains. The olives were picked and transported to the press where they were laid out on a platform and crushed by a heavy roller. The oil ran via channels into a vat. This first press, the highest quality, called virgin oil, was used for dips and cooking. The pulp was then put into baskets and again pressed. This time the oil was of inferior quality and was used for fuel for lamps as well as soaps and ointments. With the end of the olive season it was time to plant the grain crops again.

The harvest season then lasted from April to November. Spring was the time for grains, summer for grapes, and autumn for olives. Winter, with its wet season, was the time for growing. The rainwater was also collected and stored in cisterns and used during the hot summer. The autumn harvest was the most important because it generally signaled the completion of the yearly harvest. What followed were the times of the harvest celebrations. These celebrations brought the major agricultural activities to an end. These celebrations, similar to the European Oktoberfest, and Christian Christmas seasons, were times when the food supply was at its height. These celebrations, beginning with Pentecost and going through November with the harvests of different crops, provided the peasant with the opportunity of enhanced food supply and caloric intake, and a general time of happiness. It was a period when society reveled in the abundance of goods before the winter months, when stored food had to be consumed. The festivals or celebrations, while religious, originally started out as agricultural feasts coinciding with this abundance.

The poor farmer lived mainly on bread, while those who could afford fruits, especially figs and vegetables, would supplement their diet. The caloric and dietary supplements of figs, dates, almonds, onions, legumes, and pomegranates would add to the general health of the family. The region of Galilee was more fertile and allowed harvests to be later.

Vines were not only planted in the local gardens, often growing in the courtyard, but as commercial enterprises. Planted on the hills, the land had to first be prepared by terracing. Although it required a high amount of labor and investment, the returns were also quite large, often 15 times more profitable than an equal amount of land cultivated with grains. The hill was first terraced, with the rocks being removed and used as walls for protection and to reduce the soil runoff. After preparing the hill, the vines were planted and then required heavy maintenance, including watering, pruning, hoeing, weeding, and tying branches. To ensure that animals and thieves did not destroy or damage the investment, the owner often had watchtowers constructed for lookouts.

The grapes were placed in an upper basin where the fruit was pressed, running into a lower vat where it remained overnight to allow the sediment to settle. It was then put into amphora and allowed to ferment. It was stored in caves or underground, where the fermentation continued, and kept at a constant temperature. After a few months the hole in the amphora was sealed and marked, indicating the owner or type or both. A second pressing was also made from the crushed skins and made into a separate inferior quality of wine.

Flocks

The farmer often kept sheep and goats for milk, meat, wool, or hair. Unlike cattle, which require more substantial grazing areas, sheep and goats are able to exist without shelter and can obtain food in marginal conditions. Most families probably owned a few sheep and goats. During the first century shepherds probably no longer lived exclusively in the fields but rather became more settled. Living in or near their villages, shepherds had a sense of permanency. By living in villages they could pen their sheep and goats in nearby pastures. This would also allow them to be hired out as day laborers when needed, especially during the harvest season, by wealthy landowners. The shepherds after harvest would move their herds to the mountains for the hot summer. Their life, even when they became semi-nomadic, was not easy. They had to constantly watch over their flocks to prevent attacks from robbers or wild animals. They used their staff and a sling for protection. At night they gathered the sheep into sheepfolds made of stone walls or a cave, or even a valley. They might have had even a dog for help. Sleeping with their flock in all kinds of weather made their life hard and difficult. Popular opinion held the shepherd to be lowly, uncouth, and on a level with thieves.

Often a family, especially one who was nomadic, could have a flock of sheep and goats intermixed. Moving from watering hole to watering hole, these nomads had their livelihood tied up in their flocks. This movement was tied to the annual rainfall and temperature, moving from the hilltops to the desert when the latter had received rainfall.

Although requiring more land and water, cattle and oxen, at least judging by the references in the Bible and elsewhere, seem to have been more numerous than they are today. Due to changes in the ecosystem, modern support of cattle is less than in antiquity. Most villages could not support herds outside of the Transjordan and Galilee, where the land was lush and green. But because the sacrifices were important, it is likely that a wealthy individual had some cattle and that they were used by the village. Cattle nevertheless were a luxury item, used only occasionally.

In the non-Jewish regions and groups pigs were also kept. Like sheep and goats, herds of pigs were known throughout antiquity. While considered unclean by Jews, gentiles ate pork and it was a commodity easily sold and cured. Unlike cattle, which when slaughtered produced a large quantity of meat requiring a large number of participants, pigs that were slaughtered provided a smaller, more manageable amount of meat. Hence a farmer might be able to have some meat without producing a large surplus leading to spoilage.

Animal Products

The major benefit of sheep of course was wool. The shearing of sheep allowed the commodity to be a renewable source. Weaving was usually done in the home by women, although papyri from Egypt clearly show that it could also be a commercial business. The raw wool was first spun into yarn. Using a hand-held spindle, the mass of wool was turned into yarn by spinning the fibers together. Because spinning required no elaborate machine or space, it could be done anytime, anywhere, and by almost anyone.

The yarn was then often plied or twisted together, which allowed for strength, again using a spindle, which had a weight called a spindle whorl. The strands, in order to prevent tangles, were threaded through loops on a spinning bowl. At this point yarn could be dyed with a variety of colors.

Once the yarn was dyed it was now ready to be woven. The loom had vertical rows of yarns called the warp held by weights at the bottom, usually holding 10 strands each. The weaver then threaded the weft or woof, the horizontal rows, on top and bottom of the warp yarns, which then formed the weave. Once a piece of cloth was made it could be cut and sewn together with other pieces of different colors or shapes.

Another type of cloth is linen, made not from animal hair but from the flax plant. Grown in wet areas such as marshes and irrigated bottom land, the flax plant was expensive. Because linen was hard to come by, it was not worn by the peasants but wealthy individuals and the priests. Again the linen fibers could be dyed a variety of colors.

Dyes came from many sources. Red could be made from pomegranate rinds, while yellow came from saffron and safflowers. Copper ore, because of its characteristic green, was widely used. Black came from hematite, the main ore of iron. The murex mollusks, along the Phoenician coast, produced expensive dyes from red purple to blue purple to blue. They were only used in the Temple and worn by the ultra-elite. It is estimated that 10,000 mollusks would be needed to dye one garment, hence its high cost. The Phoenicians, especially Tyre, owned the monopoly for producing this dye.

The average family of course did not produce linen or richly colored clothes. Instead they wove what was needed into utilitarian garments. Jesus' robe was supposedly valued because it was in one piece, judging by the stories, meaning that the workmanship was superior to normal robes used by most people. Goat hair was prized for its strength and was used for tents, sacks, and ropes; it was not usually worn as clothing.

Another product from raising animals, especially goats, sheep, and cattle, was leather. Leather was used for tentmaking and sacks. The skins were sent to a tannery where they were first cleaned with water and then had the hair removed. This could be accomplished with harsh chemicals or by scrapping the skin with a knife. The skins were then treated with animal fat, egg yolks or other oils, or even urine. This would allow the skins to not stiffen and rot. After this process the skins were then ready for tanning. First the skin was rubbed with dung to allow the tannins to penetrate—using dog dung allows the natural enzymes in the feces to digest the collagen, and this allows the skin to lay flat. After this process the hide was washed to remove the smelly dung. Using tannins from the oak bark and water, the hide was soaked and then allowed to dry. This produced leather, which could be cut to the desired size. They could also use the brains of the animal to tan the hide as well, although this required more work and time. After the leather was prepared, it could then be used for a variety of uses. The New Testament makes reference to Paul as a tentmaker. Tents would have been made with the end-product of the leather-making process.

Day Workers

Local peasants also supplemented their work outside their own farmsteads. In the New Testament there are examples of day workers, who probably were a mixture of nonfarm workers, often seasonal, and farm owners who hired themselves out to local landowners (Matt. 20:1–16). These larger estates, which had their own slaves and tenants, also employed seasonal laborers because it was more economical (Matt. 21:33–41). The estate owner did not need to have a large number of workers employed or sustained during the off months; it was cheaper to hire the workers and pay them for a short period of time. The local peasant probably found this type of work an important component of his economic livelihood. An example of a large estate mentioned in the Gospels is related in the parable of the workers who were hired to work in the vineyards (Matt. 20:1–16). While the message of the story is not crucial for this example, it does show that the idea of being available for daily work was common and that the owner would hire seasonal workers.

Sabbath

An important component of ancient Jewish society was the first fruits, an offering to God. This was a tithe, which literally means one-tenth of the produce, and was limited to wheat, barley, grapes (wine), figs, pomegranates, olives (olive oil), and dates. Other vegetables were later included in the tithes. Later rabbinical literature exempted produce from the corners of the fields, wastelands, and unowned crops from the tithes and instead mandated that they be used for the poor. Of course any crop from a non-Jew was likewise exempt. Each crop had to be individually tithed without balancing the others out. The separation process required an individual to be ritually clean and required that the entire process conformed to religious law.

Although not directly associated with the first fruits, but clearly with agriculture, was the sabbatical year. According to this law, one year out of seven farmers should allow their land to lie fallow. This followed the concept of the weekly Sabbath. The fields benefited from the rest because they were not exploited and drained of important nutrients. This practice, however, required the farmer to have enough supplies stored for use during the sabbatical year. This would often require hardships, because a poor harvest often hit the farmer twice, once during the bad harvest and then again for the sabbatical year when produce would be low.

In the Greek regions of Palestine and Syria, the day-to-day activities were similar to those of the Jewish inhabitants, except for the religious tenets. As the early followers of Christianity moved into and converted inhabitants in Asia Minor and Greece, there were some changes. In these regions the level of Jewish followers was markedly lower, and as such, the number of religious taboos decreased. For examples, pigs were no longer forbidden due to the lack of enforcement of the Jewish dietary laws. The local peasants in these regions continued to operate their farms as they had done for the past millennium.

A WOMAN'S STORY

During the Bar Kohba war of 132–135 C.E. at En-Gedi, a region centered on the Western shore of the Dead Sea, a Jewish woman Babatha, daughter of Simon, and second wife of Judah, son of Elazar Khrthousion, a leading family, fled into the caves three miles south (for a full discussion see Anthony J Saldarini, "Babatha's Story," *Biblical Archaeology Review,* 24 (1998): 28–39). Two groups sought refuge in two caves and were ultimately starved out by the Romans. Babatha carried her possessions, including her family papers into the caves. Realizing that she would not escape, or at least not escape with her belongings, she hid them in the cave, probably with the hope of returning for them once she got away. This hoard has given us an insight into her life and the family.

Babatha's documents show that she was a daughter of Simon from Maoz and by 124 she was a young widow with a son, Jesus, son of Jesus. In 128 she married Judah, who already had a wife, Miriam, and a daughter, Shelamzion. Judah died in 130 and the latest document is dated 132 at the beginning of the war and the earliest is dated 94.

The archive shows what life was like in a small community and village or city in Israel. Most of the documents are legal, but they show business connections including relations with Roman officials in Rabbat, Moab, and Petra.

The documents indicate that property lines were clearly established between neighbors and that the transfer of property was carefully recorded. Babatha had date palm orchards, houses, courtyards, a 400 denarii trust fund, a loan of 500 denarii, deposits, and other property. These documents show that she was a woman of financial means and that the area around the Dead Sea was not economically barren. Babatha was probably typical of the regions elites. Of the 35 documents, 26 were written in Greek, 6 in Nabatean, and

3 in Aramaic. In the Greek documents only one person, Babatha's son Jesus, is clearly identified as a Jew. Why was he identified as such? It may have been that people were only identified as Jews when it was not obvious, for example, converts, proselytes, gentiles who observe Jewish customs, or perhaps a proper name. He was not a proselyte and since he was a minor and this was a legal document, his identification as a Jew was a legal issue. The Greek documents show that the contract used was in the prevailing legal system of the time. There were official legal documents that show things such as the stipulations about the formal court questions and answers about a business transaction.

The document about Babatha's son's guardianship shows the influence of Roman law. She could not be her son's guardian, so the Petra's council appointed two men; Jewish law would have allowed her to be guardian if her husband had appointed her, but he did not, so she now used Roman law to protect her. She argued that the guardians had not been conscientious and in fact had not behaved properly. Although the case's outcome is not clear, it appears that seven years later she was still arguing the point, and had not received the proper amount for her son's maintenance and inheritance.

In both Babatha's documents and others, Greek norms exist. A marriage contract commits the husband to clothe and feed his wives and children according to Greek customs. But in Babatha's own Aramaic contract, Judah marries her according to the "laws of Moses and the Jews." Another marriage contract from another Jewish archive has support for the wife and child only if the husband dies, not a Greek law but a Jewish one. In essence both Jewish and Greek laws were used interchangeably. The laws of the village were also followed, called the "Law of the Jews" in Aramaic and "Greek Customs" in Greek.

The archive shows no rabbinic law or Jewish religious laws. The Mishnaic and Talmudic religious laws with their strict observance were not mentioned. Her Aramaic marriage contract said she could continue to live in the house and be supported by Judah's heirs or could be sent away if her dowry was returned. The documents show no distinction among the different social groups: Nabatean, Roman, Greek, or Jew. The tensions between Jews and Gentiles are not seen in these documents and neither are the political groups, destruction of the Temple, or the Messiah. Rather, the archive shows prosperous Jews living in peace with their Gentile neighbors. They observe Jewish and local customs and cooperate and live within the Roman system. Since Babatha did not recover her documents, we can assume she did not return to the cave. We have no idea what happened to her.

URBAN LIFE

Markets

For villages without a synagogue, the inhabitants would travel to the nearest town for services. These services, held on Monday and Thursday, corresponded to the market days and the two were therefore connected. The local peasants, needing both worship and sustenance, would receive both on the same days placed three to four days apart. The situation in the local towns where markets existed provided for local protection. The town usually had some sort of wall and gates that could be closed and protected by a tower. Coming into a town through the gate, one would enter the square from which streets radiated out. This square provided the marketplace for both town folks and rural inhabitants, who could engage in commerce, discussion, and even rebellion. The merchants would set up their stalls and sell their wares. The country dwellers would bring in their produce to sell, while the traveling merchant could ply his trade. Depending on the town, wares could have traveled from throughout the Mediterranean, allowing the buyer to wear the most recent type of clothing or own the latest style of cookware. Merchants from the East, Alexandria, Athens, and Rome not only sold their produce but shared gossip. These marketplaces became sites where information freely passed. Included in this mix were the *publicani,* the tax collectors who made sure that no one evaded the local and imperial taxes. It was not uncommon for the towns to have a central fountain from which water was drawn. Here the local news could be spread.

In the evening the town continued to have life. Night watchmen constantly patrolled the street to insure that no one was molested or got into trouble. Windows from the nearby houses allowed light from within to shine out, usually having lattices and grates. Outside there were torches that lit the way for those walking about at night.

Town Structures and Government

Jewish towns included Greek structures, which the locals used. For example, baths became more common. The Jewish teacher Gamaliel, Paul's teacher, supposedly said, upon frequenting a bath with the statue of Venus, that the statue adorned the bath and not the bath the statue, indicating that it was acceptable to use. In Egypt a fourth-century papyrus detailed the description of an Egyptian town and its watchmen, indicating which streets they patrolled. This reflected the situation throughout the Roman Empire. The papyrus (P.Oxy. 48) is interesting in that it mentions a Christian church along with the other pagan temples and the meeting house or basilica. It is probable that many Jewish towns, especially in Galilee, which had only recently been converted, still retained a large pagan population.

Jewish towns were controlled by a variety of officials. For example, the Romans had ultimate authority, even though they did not have a continuous presence. Within a town of 120 men there was the Sanhedrim or council, which consisted of 23 members; for towns less than 120 men the governing board was only three. These boards were appointed by the authority of the Temple in Jerusalem, the Great Sanhedrim, which had 71 members. In addition to their religious functions, these councils probably had civil powers that allowed the towns to function. This was a familiar practice throughout the Mediterranean world. Rome preferred to govern through these councils because this allowed the locals to bear the brunt of complaints about tax collecting and enforcing imperial rules. There was also a town president or mayor who was responsible for the day-to-day running of the city and relating information to and from the governor's office.

The cities and towns had rules and officers in charge of protection, most notably sanitation, because the spread of disease had to be prevented. In Caesarea on the shoreline, Josephus informs us that there were sewage drains leading into the sea for waste removal. In towns there must have been similar systems. Outside the city or town proper were the cemeteries. Ancient societies placed them there because of the taboo against the dead remaining in the cities.

Travel

Often outside the towns on the roads were the *khans,* local inns or hostels. Many of these were merely a large courtyard in the middle for the animals and carts, with rooms opening onto the courtyard. They were unfurnished and provided a rudimentary place to sleep. Although payment was not expected, an individual would often oversee the place and for a fee could get the traveler food, drink, and other amenities. These places were usually for the stranger or foreigner. For the traveler living in the region, hospitality was expected. Numerous references in the Talmud indicate that the rabbis believed that hospitality was an important necessity. The hosts would meet and accompany their guest, providing for their lodging, food, and entertainment. Part of this philosophy came from the religious ideology that the travelers could be angels, and one should not offend God or his messengers.

The roads throughout the Roman Empire were of varying grades and oversight. Some roads were maintained by the imperial government at great cost and regularity. Numerous milestones and markers indicate that the military and other entities, in the name of the emperors, repaired, improved, and extended the roads. From manuscripts and papyri it is known that there were official stations placed at regular intervals. These stations, primarily for the imperial agents, provided places for changing horses, getting supplies, sleeping quarters, and protection. For the local community these stations provided a link with the central government, and more importantly the army. There were roads that were serviced by the local communities. Again certain rules, such as ensuring that there were no overhanging branches, removal of dead animals, or cleaning of rubbish at regular intervals were written down and presumably enforced. Many of these rules also indicated the width and repair cycles. The Talmud indicated that public roads were to be 24 feet wide with no underground structures, to ensure safety. Finally there were some roads that were little more than paths, which tended to not be maintained or have any real amenities.

For the peasant living in Palestine during the first century C.E., there were constant needs for movement and travel. While some may not have had the need to move about the region in a nomadic lifestyle such as did shepherds or goat herders, many did travel, if only to go to a nearby market or to Jerusalem for the festivals. There were many dangers associated with this travel. The parable of the man robbed and beaten on the roadway that Jesus told must have been a common enough event for the audience to understand. The fact that there was an inn that the Samaritan took the traveler to must have also been common enough. What also lends support to the idea that travel was common can be seen in the matter-of-fact presentation of Jesus and his disciples traveling throughout Palestine. This is further supported by the idea that in the Talmud (Pes. 93b) an ordinary trip could be as far as 40 Roman miles or about 36½ modern miles. One assumed that this was probably not by foot but rather by cart or beast. The great festival in Jerusalem brought travelers flocking the roads to and from the capital. In the Gospel of Luke it is clear that this travel was communal, with pilgrims traveling as a group. The importance of the pilgrimage was central during this time and provided an avenue for vacations and distractions.

Pilgrimages

The pilgrimage was first and foremost religious. During the period of the New Testament Jews living around Jerusalem traveled to the Temple weekly. Those living in Palestine but not close enough to travel weekly were expected to go yearly. The story in Luke of Jesus and his family going to the Temple when he was 12 would be an example (Luke 2:41–51). For those who lived outside of Palestine it was expected that one would travel to the Temple at least once in their lifetime. This religious journey was meant to renew one's faith and provide the connection between God and the individual. But the pilgrimage was also a chance to travel, to see the different sites. Jews outside Palestine viewed this opportunity to see the land where the their ancestors, Abraham, Moses, David, and Solomon, all existed. The journey allowed one to make business connections, renew friendships, and make contacts with important members of the Jewish community. The pilgrimage was also a vacation, a chance to explore the world. For the peasant, the pilgrimage allowed them to leave their locale and explore another region or regions. While it is hard to determine if peasants from Egypt, Greece, or Italy could make the once-in-a-lifetime journey, it is clear that the idea of a pilgrimage made an impact.

During the post–New Testament period, after the destruction of Jerusalem, Christians continued to view the pilgrimage as important. Evidence exists that clearly shows that traveling to Jerusalem was still one of the most important journeys one could make. The account of an anonymous traveler from Gaul (France) recounts the journey in the early fourth century C.E. to Jerusalem. The work describes the journey and sites, but its main importance is the description of Jerusalem around the year 400 C.E. The following is the section on Jerusalem and takes into account not only what one would have seen at the time but the general history.

THE CITY OF JERUSALEM

Jerusalem
Thence to Jerusalem—12 miles.
Total from Caesarea Palaestina to Jerusalem 116 miles, 4 halts, 4 changes.

There are in Jerusalem two large pools (piscinae) at the side of the temple (ad latus templi), that is, one upon the right hand, and one upon the left, which were made by Solomon; and further in the city are twin pools (piscinae gemellares), with five porticoes, which are called Bethsaida (John 5:2–18). There persons who have been sick for many years are cured; the pools contain water which is red when it is disturbed. There is also here a crypt, in which Solomon used to torture devils.

Here is also the corner of an exceeding high tower, where our Lord ascended and the tempter said to Him, "If thou be the Son of God, cast thyself down from hence" (Matt 4:7). And the Lord answered, "Thou shalt not tempt the Lord thy God, but him only shalt thou serve" (Matt 4:10). There is a great corner-stone, of which it was said, "The stone which the builders rejected is become the head of the corner" (Matt 21:42; Ps 118:22). Under the pinnacle (pinna) of the tower are many rooms, and here was Solomon's palace. There also is the chamber in which he sate and wrote the (Book of) Wisdom; this chamber is covered with a single stone. There are also large subterranean reservoirs for water and pools constructed with great labour. And in the building (in aede) itself, where stood the temple which Solomon built, they say that the blood of Zacharias (Matt 23:35; Luke 11:51) which was shed upon the stone pavement before the altar remains to this day. There are also to be seen the marks of the nails in the shoes of the soldiers who slew him, throughout the whole enclosure, so plain that you would think they were impressed upon wax. There are two statues of Hadrian, and not far from the statues there is a perforated stone, to which the Jews come every year and anoint it, bewail themselves with groans, rend their garments, and so depart. There also is the house of Hezekiah King of Judah.

Also as you come out of Jerusalem to go up Mount Sion, on the left hand, below in the valley, beside the wall, is a pool which is called Siloe (John 9:7) and has four porticoes; and there is another large pool outside it. This spring runs for six days and nights, but on the seventh day, which is the Sabbath, it does not run at all, either by day or by night. On this side one goes up Sion, and sees where the house of Caiaphas the priest was, and there still stands a column against which Christ was beaten with rods. Within, however, inside the wall of Sion, is seen the place where was David's palace. Of seven synagogues which once were there, one alone remains; the rest are ploughed over and sown upon, as said Isaiah the prophet (Is 1:8; Michah 3:12).

From thence as you go out of the wall of Sion, as you walk towards the gate of Neapolis, towards the right, below in the valley, are walls, where was the house or praetorium of Pontius Pilate (Matt 27:27). Here our Lord was tried before His passion. On the left hand is the little hill of Golgotha where the Lord was crucified (Matt 27:33). About a stone's throw from thence is a vault (crypta) wherein His body was laid, and rose again on the third day (Matt 27:63; 28:6). There, at present, by the command of the Emperor Constantine (iussu Constantini), has been built a basilica, that is to say, a church (dominicum) of wondrous beauty, having at the side reservoirs (excepturia) from which water is raised, and a bath behind in which infants are washed (baptized).

Also as one goes from Jerusalem to the gate which is to the eastward, in order to ascend the Mount of Olives, is the valley called that of Josaphat. Towards the left, where are vineyards, is a stone at the place where Judas Iscariot betrayed Christ (Matt. 26:47–50); on the right is a palm-tree, branches of which the children carried off and strewed in the way when Christ came (Matt 31:8). Not far from thence, about a stone's-throw, are two notable tombs of wondrous beauty; in the one, which is a true monolith, lies Isaiah the prophet, and in the other Hezekiah, King of the Jews.

From thence you ascend to the Mount of Olives, where before the Passion, the Lord taught His disciples (Matt 24–25). There by the orders of Constantine a basilica of wondrous beauty has been built. Not far from thence is the little hill which the Lord ascended to pray, when he took Peter and John with Him, and Moses and Elias were beheld (Matt 17:1–8).

Source: Itinerary from Bordeaux to Jerusalem (330 C.E.) translation by Aubrey Stewart (London: Committee of the Palestine Exploration Fund, 1887), 589–596.

8

FAMILY LIFE AND LIVING CONDITIONS

Jesus said to her, Go, call your husband, and come here. The woman answered and said, I have no husband. Jesus said to her, You have well said I have no husband, for you have had five husbands, and the one whom you now have is not your husband; in that you spoke truly. (John 4:16–18)

Individuals mentioned in the New Testament came from all walks of life with different influences and histories. This chapter examines how individuals living during the time of the New Testament lived and what their living conditions were.

MARRIAGE

During the New Testament era marriage and family life were the mainstay of society. Although family life could exist without marriage, the institution was and remained the backbone of family life. The New Testament, supplemented with other works, provides glimpses into family life and society, in which marriage formed the basis of most social interactions. During the Roman Republic, when a son took a wife she passed out of her father's control and into his, which the Romans termed *manus* (meaning "hand"). In the late Republic a new form of marriage, *sine manus* (without hand or power transferred) allowed the bride to remain under her father's control and hence gave her the right to inherit. This in turn meant that she had some independence from her husband because she was not completely under his economic control. In the *sine manus* form of marriage the husband received the dowry, which he could use but again it was held under certain limitations. During the time of the New Testament this form of marriage was common not only in Roman society but in Greek society as well.

In Jewish society the traditional form of marriage existed, but even it was undergoing change, moving more toward the Greek and Roman view. What is important to remember about these marriage forms is that they were fluid depending upon the social and economic status of the families. For the wealthy and powerful the families wanted to ensure that they received the most advantageous position for their own family. For example, the bride's family might want to insist on a marriage *sine manus* because it gave her power and the means to maintain her independence. The groom's family might demand in exchange a larger dowry to offset their loss of power. Traditionally the dowry provided income-producing property or goods that sustained the couple. It was therefore crucial to the groom's family that the dowry be large enough to provide not only for the couple but their children as well. During the early Empire a new addition to the marriage contract was a gift *(donation)* from the groom's family to the bride, which ultimately exceeded the value of the dowry. This practice could cause problems for the groom's family because many young men did not have the means to provide a large gift. The bride's family of course welcomed this change, which relieved them of the burden of providing a large dowry. This change from a large bride's dowry to a large groom's gift in turn delayed marriage for the men, while the bride's family wanted to make an arrangement when she was young. For poor families the dowry and gift were still observed but they were not as important. It is more likely that during this period poorer individuals were able to marry for love, while wealthy individuals married because of family ambitions.

What is most striking about the ancient marriage is its business-like function, seen in the marriage contract. The contract made marriage more like a business acquisition or merger of two companies, especially when it involved members of the aristocracy or mercantile class. This contract placed requirements on both sides of the marriage parties and was meant to protect both partners, their families, and society. Marriage contracts were common throughout the Mediterranean ancient world, beginning with prebiblical societies and continuing throughout antiquity well into the modern era. The goal of the contract was to allow the union not only of individuals but other elements of society, including economic, political, and social forces.

Jewish Marriage

In the New Testament era the major social unit was the traditional Jewish marriage (John 2:1–11). The ancient Jewish customs for the marriage began with the *shiddukhin,* or the match. This was usually initiated by the groom's father, although a matchmaker was often employed, and it required the consent of the bride. This was common in non-Jewish societies as well. After the match was made, the *mohar* or bride price was paid as was required by Jewish law. It was paid by the groom's father or the groom if he was of age, and originally reflected the value of the bride. During the first century C.E. the price seems to have been 100 *denarii,* a sizable sum, equivalent to a pound of silver or four gold coins, or 100 days of labor for a common workman. The *mattan,* or love gifts, although not required, were given by the groom to the bride and showed his love for her. The *shiluhim,* or dowry, was then given by the bride's father, allowing her to be supported, and this was part of her inheritance. The *ketubah* or actual marriage contract was now drawn up. It was a written document stating the value of the *mohar* and detailed the rights the bride would have and the requirements or promises made by the groom.

Once the contract was made the *kiddushin* or betrothal took place. The betrothal could last up to a year, and it seems that the couple could live together, even having sexual relations. This fact may account for the story in the New Testament in which Joseph, hearing Mary was pregnant even though they had not had sexual relations, planned to put her aside. The point of the story is not that sex was out of the question, but rather that Mary's child was not Joseph's. Finally the *nissuin* or wedding took place when the groom's father decided that the time was right. It was traditionally seen as the unexpected arrival of the groom who now "abducted the bride" and married her. Many of these ideas existed in other societies as well and probably went back to early periods. For example, the "abduction of the bride" existed in both Greek and Roman cultures.

The most important social component was the dowry. The dowry paid by the bride's father was given to the groom to use to support the wife and family, but he could not abuse or squander it. It is often viewed as the price paid by the bride's family to the groom, but it really was meant to provide the bride with protection, especially if something happened to the groom. In classical times the dowry, especially if it was money or land, would be used by the husband, but he was responsible for maintaining its value. Often the dowry consisted of furniture, clothing, dishes, or other items not readily identifiable as income-producing. If a divorce occurred the dowry could be required to be returned to the wife, or if a court decided that the wife was at fault it might be forfeited to the husband. If the wife died the dowry could be returned to her family or held as part of her children's inheritance. The dowry, then, should not be seen as a fee paid to the groom to marry the woman, but rather as an economic component to ensure that the bride's family continued. Often the size of the dowry depended on the bride's family position and aspirations. If her family desired her to marry into a family more connected, powerful, or financially successful, then they might increase the amount of her dowry to make the match more acceptable and appealing. The marriage contract spelled out all of the parameters concerning the dowry and was similar to, but not exactly like modern prenuptial agreements.

The marriage contract also detailed what provisions were to be made concerning heirs. This was important for determining what became of the family estate, especially because both parties realized that one of them might die and the other remarry. For example, if the husband and wife had two children, the contract might say that half of the estate was guaranteed for their children, in this case 25 percent each, with the rest going to the survivor. That way if the wife died and the husband remarried, their children were protected if he had future children. Likewise if a husband or wife married again and brought into the marriage children, they would be provided for or explicitly stated not to be recognized in the will. These contracts often make the institution of marriage seem like a business, and in a sense it was, because it attempted to protect all involved and take into account different contingencies. It is possible that there were standardized marriage contracts that one simply requested from a scribe or lawyer. The scribe then merely wrote in the particulars but the standard format was the same.

DIVORCE

In the New Testament period divorce was also common. While the ancient world favored the husband, often with a double standard, women by the time of Jesus had certain rights. In the Hellenistic and Roman world women could initiate divorce, although any children remained with the husband. In the Old Testament period Judaism had also allowed divorce, which again could only be initiated by the husband; the wife or others could try to compel him to file for a divorce if she wanted it, but he was under no obligation. Before Hillel, the first-century B.C.E. rabbi who lived during the reign of Herod the Great, a man could divorce his wife only on the grounds of his not fulfilling the three obligations in the book of Exodus 21:10ff, providing his wife food, clothing, or love. If a man failed to provide his wife with these three obligations he or she, usually with help from her family, could divorce. Although technically only a man in Judaism could write a divorce certificate, women ultimately could do it as well, especially through a scribe or by persuading a male guardian in her family.

Hillel, however, argued that divorce could also proceed based on Deuteronomy 24:1, which originally was viewed as "a matter of indecency." If a wife was found to be indecent, that is, if she committed adultery, the husband could divorce her. But Hillel viewed Deuteronomy 24:1 as two separate issues, indecency and as "a matter." The latter in essence meant that Jewish men, like their Greek counterparts, could divorce for any reason. Judaism had been exposed to outside influences over the past six centuries, which in turn had constantly made an impact on its social fabric. After the Persian Empire (500 B.C.E.), which had a history of concubines, and the Hellenistic or Greek influence, which had similarly subjected women to an inferior status, the Jewish institution of marriage had been under constant attack. Hellenistic and then later Roman philosophy allowed for divorce, especially among the upper class, for any reason. The Greek influences within Palestine was what led to this debate in Judaism and Hillel's ultimate teaching. This interpretation may be seen in the Gospel (Mark 10:2–9; Matt. 19:1–9) when Jesus, when asked about divorce, does not mention the three obligations allowed in Exodus. Even though this was the standard Jewish reason for divorce, as he grew up in a society where divorce was allowed along the lines of Exodus, Jesus limited divorce to a "matter of decency," that is, the traditional reading of Deuteronomy 24:1, but not the new ideas of Hillel that included both indecency and "any matter" or "any cause." In other words, Jesus did not advocate the no-fault divorce current in Judaism, which had been advocated by Hillel. That Jesus did not mention divorce for the three obligations does not mean that Jesus was against divorce; rather, his failure to mention the three obligations merely showed that Jesus was not altering the Torah and the traditional views of Judaism. In addition Jesus did not object to the idea of "a matter of decency" in Deuteronomy. In this latter point Jesus was not alone since the Sammaites, a Jewish sect, believed in the same thing.

Although the traditional Jewish view is that only the man could initiate divorce, some scholars have argued that this traditional view is incorrect. The Pharisees during the first and second centuries C.E. taught against women initiating divorce, which some scholars argue indicates that it was actually occurring. The proof for this contradiction comes from several Jewish sources throughout their history. In Egypt at Elephantine during the Persian period, local records of a Jewish community indicate that Jewish women could initiate divorce. The traditional view concerning this period is that this sect was separated and isolated from the Temple and its religious leadership in Jerusalem. But recent arguments have shown that during the Persian period Jewish citizens in Egypt were in regular contact with the leaders of the Temple in Jerusalem and yet still allowed for the wife to initiate divorce. In the Gospel of Mark 10:11–12, Jesus said if a man divorces his wife and remarries he commits adultery, and if she divorces her husband and marries another she commits adultery. The accepted view is that Mark was writing for the Greek audience, which allowed divorce. While this may be true, Mark nevertheless could not state ideas that were alien to Judaism just to appease a non-Jewish audience, because many of Mark's audiences would have known the Jewish community as well. The passage then clearly shows that women could initiate divorce in the first century C.E. in Judaism. Finally, a papyrus from the 140s C.E. indicates that a wife could divorce as well. This papyrus is a written notification similar to the many already existing papyri from men who initiated divorce.

During the New Testament period, then, women could divorce according to both Jewish law and customs similar to their Greco-Roman counterparts. For the early Christians their task was how the new religion based in Jewish customs but operating in the Greco-Roman world could address this issue. Paul in 1 Corinthians 7 followed Jesus' view in rejecting Hillel's "any matter" cause and the Greek practice of separating from each other and returning the dowry. Paul dealt with the issue of divorce by declaring that a Christian should not just end the marriage, even if the spouse was a pagan. If two Christians could not remain married he urged them to remain single after the divorce in case they might be reconciled. But if one was a nonbeliever the Church had no hold over the couple, unlike in the case of both being believers. Paul declared they would be no longer bound. Of course this is the crux of the issue, whether this meant they were no longer bound to live with the partner but still unable to remarry, or no longer married meaning they could remarry. Probably it meant that they were no longer married and were thus free to remarry. Paul clearly went beyond Jesus' view that divorce for the three obligations in Exodus was allowed, and he probably was attempting to fight against the Greco-Roman prevalence of easy divorce. Paul may in fact have believed in the Exodus views but was attempting not to confuse his followers who were not knowledgeable in Jewish customs and laws. This attempt to discourage divorce clearly shows that divorce and remarriage existed in the early Church. The Church attempted to get a handle on it in order to prevent the Christians from falling into the same camp as other mystery religions in the Mediterranean world and thus losing their uniqueness.

FAMILY

While there were numerous motives as to why two people should marry, for most the major purpose of marriage was to begin a family and create a household. The Roman name for family, *familia,* like the Greek term *oikos* (household; ancient Greek did not have a term for family), meant more than just the parent-children unit, it meant the entire household. Likewise in Palestine this system was also in place. It is important to realize that the family unit was more than just the nuclear family. A poor family might have the parents, unmarried children, a sister, brother's widow, or grandmother. The role here was to provide not only for the nuclear family but the nearby extended family, in particular those individuals who could not take care of themselves, that is, unmarried/widowed women. For a family with more resources the household might include a few servants, both free and slaves, who were usually regarded as members of the household. The New Testament mentions one the servant or slave of the chief priest whom Peter attacked when Jesus was seized (John 18:10). This person, and others like him, were extensions of the family. If they were slaves and later freed they often continued to be viewed as family members. For the wealthy households there were numerous servants and other extended family members who often remained as part of the household indefinitely. These individuals, who otherwise could establish their own households, remained as part of the household to ensure their level of comfort, protect the household estate, and provide support for the family's leadership.

This household was more than just a family; it served as a social, political, economic, and religious structure for society. Socially the family made up part of a larger unit: in Roman society the *gens,* in Jewish society the tribe. These units often joined together for mutual aid. At the top of the household, Greek, Roman, or Jewish, stood the father, the Roman *paterfamilias,* who had absolute control over all of those in his household. He had the power to accept or reject any newborn child, slave, wife, or servant, and his power extended to all aspects of their lives. The *paterfamilias* controlled the family's religious practices. In pagan Rome the *paterfamilias* performed the sacrifices. He also dispensed family justice; in fact he originally had the power to execute family members. With his death his adult sons received equal shares of the estate and became their own *paterfamilias.* As time went on the power of the *paterfamilias* was limited. During the Roman Republic the returning soldiers with their plunder kept it and used it to break away from the domineering power of the *paterfamilias.* In addition, his power to execute family members also disappeared. Nevertheless, during the time of the New Testament the power of the father was still important, especially for those who were rich and powerful.

In antiquity laws and customs favored the male. Adultery in Roman and Greek society, and to a great extent Jewish, was only a crime for the woman. The man was typically free to engage in relations as he wished, and in households with slave girls masters could do as they wish. The woman, on the other hand, could be killed or, after the time of Emperor Augustus, fined based on her dowry. During the Empire a wife who was wronged could recover her dowry. Adultery only became a crime on an equal basis for both sexes during the reign of Constantine. Homosexuality, particularly in the Greek and Roman world, but not as much in Judaism, existed and was not criminalized, and in wealthy households slave boys were abused for their master's pleasures.

The family also served as the basis of the political power within society. While it is commonplace now for individuals to side with a particular political party, in ancient society one's family views usually held sway. This was in part due to the institution of patronage. During the Republic and early Empire wealthy individuals, not only in Rome but throughout the Roman world, practiced patronage. A wealthy individual would have a variety of clients who supported him in his political, social, or economic endeavors, in return for maintenance. This maintenance could be protection, food, money, or social support. This institution of patronage produced a system in which individuals were all tied together to ensure that society functioned. The relationship between client and master could be contentious or placid depending upon the individuals and the situations. The clients had a personal connection, which in turn made the political actions personal. Hence when one reads about the Herodians, it does not completely mean the party of Herod but can also mean his and his family's clients, those who followed Herod because of his patronage.

The family also served as the economic basis of society. In antiquity, seen in the New Testament, there were a variety of economic forces that affected the family. While most of the inhabitants, upwards of 75 percent, engaged in agriculture there were merchants, tradesmen, skilled laborers, and professionals. The family in most of these instances was the economic center for these occupations. While farms may have been of varying sizes, they were nevertheless controlled by a family. Even large estates were owned by a family, although they could be managed by others. The idea of a large corporation running an agro-business was not unheard of but was still unusual. The family, as witnessed by numerous papyri found in Egypt, kept detailed accounts of the running of the estate or farm. These account books often list transactions one would expect from a farm, selling and buying of goods, transporting supplies, paying of taxes. They often recorded other transactions that the modern reader might find interesting: paying bribes to soldiers, paying for services from dancers and others, and dealing with occasional problems such as cattle wandering in others' fields, thieves, and even attacks on servants. For small farms there exist accounts that likewise show similar trends but on a smaller scale. The small farm owners also had a problem with large estate owners trying to take over smaller farms.

CHILDREN

Normally one of the major goals of a marriage was the production of children. Although some marriages were arranged in which having children was not a primary object, partners in most marriages hoped that children would be born. Some families may have wanted to limit the number of children produced. Although abortions existed they were universally frowned upon and even prohibited. During the New Testament period, Jewish and, later, Christian sentiments prohibited abortions. Contraception was also practiced although without great success. In addition to oral and topical potions and inserted preparations to block fertilization, the rhythm method and spells were employed, although usually without great success.

Childbirth was a dangerous time not only for the child but for the mother. To assist in the delivery of a child, midwives were regularly employed. For most families the mother nursed the child; however, in wealthy families a wet nurse, typically a slave, was used. Some families did not want the child and infanticide was an acceptable practice. An occasional system was to deposit the newborn into a trash heap; if someone rescued the child, it could be raised as a slave or as their own. Selling unwanted babies was also allowed, although by the second and third centuries C.E. the practice was severely limited. Nevertheless, the hope for children was more common.

Family life centered on the social status of the family and their interactions with others. At the top stood the elites, in which the wife was expected to produce heirs, but outside of this duty child-rearing usually fell to the slaves and servants. Emperors, kings, and many nobles often did not have time for the usual early childhood. Many in modern society often imagine our present-day child-centered philosophy and practices extending back into antiquity. It is doubtful that Alexander the Great's mother, Olympias, spent much time with the future conqueror in any real meaningful way, yet many view his actions and choices as deeply rooted in her control over him, as if she had been the primary caregiver. In the same way many of the elites in the first century C.E. did not actively engage in the child's upbringing. For the middle class family life would have been different. Here the mother and father would have had more direct contact, and because the family would have been small with a few servants and slaves in a house accessible by all, the interactions would have been more common. Although the child would still have been nursed and cared for by a substitute, the mother and father would have been in daily contact. For the poor family, life continued to be intimate, with mother and father caring directly for the child.

Children have always been the primary function of a marriage because it allows the families' bloodlines to continue. While the rate of infant mortality was high, most families attempted to have several children. Children, when old enough, were expected to work on the farm or in the family trade. Most were given rudimentary education, usually contingent upon their societal position and income. For wealthier families the educational system was superior. Typically a child would have a tutor, either slave or freedman, who would train the students in reading, writing, and logic. For some students this was all that was necessary, while for others there would be continued studies, especially in rhetoric and the law. For those Jewish families in which the boy showed promise or whose families wanted even more specialized education, opportunities to learn from the rabbis existed. While some students continued education in religious matters, others learned the trade of their family or friends. This training, especially for mercantile settings, often required knowledge of trade routes (geography), languages and customs (negotiations), or specialized products (manufacturing). This experiential learning was crucial if the student was to be successful.

HOUSES AND SLAVES

In Palestine, wealthy families had houses that typically had three large rooms laid out to form a U, with a courtyard accessible from all three rooms and a gate that could enclose the courtyard and protect the house. Two stories high, these houses provided room for families, livestock, and supplies. For poorer families the houses were usually small, having one to six rooms, many of them doubling as living/bed rooms. With multiple generations living in the same house, families spent a great deal of their time creating boundaries. During the day most of the family would be outside working in the fields or in their shops. Meal and night times would have meant the family was more concentrated and in closer proximity.

During the time of the New Testament, as witnessed in the writings in the first century c.e., slavery not only existed, but was accepted. Slavery existed in nearly all parts of the empire. The supply of slaves during the Republic continually increased, especially after the Second Punic War (218–204 b.c.e.) when Rome annexed large portions of the East. After Julius Caesar conquered Gaul and the wars between Anthony and Octavian ended, the supply of slaves from conquest declined. Previously Roman authors, notably Cato the Elder (ca. 150 b.c.e.) advocated against slaves reproducing because they were so inexpensive to buy. With the decline in the number of slaves from wars, however, owners now often allowed slaves to reproduce. Although some wars occurred in which new slaves entered the market, most notably the Jewish rebellion of 66 c.e., most slaves now came from reproduction and piracy.

Christianity as seen in the New Testament did not advocate the elimination of slavery, which in antiquity was common and expected. In addition to being captured in war, one could become a slave through a variety of other means: being born to a slave, being exposed by parents and raised as a slave, or being a criminal. Although there was a legal separation between slavery and freedom, conditions separating the poor and slaves were not that far apart. Slaves had some legal protection, especially by the time of the Empire. They could not be executed at the whim of their master, who had to provide a reason for wanting a slave dead. Slaves could also buy their freedom, and many were granted freedom. Often the reason for this freedom was so the master did not have to take care of slaves in their old age, a practice the Emperor Augustus forbade, since it led to an increase of urban poor who might resort to criminal activities to survive. Nevertheless, when a slave was freed, so were his or her future children.

Slaves existed across the social continuum. Some poor families could afford one slave to help in the fields, while wealthy individuals could have as many as a thousand. Slaves were also employed in a wide variety of functions. Slaves performed numerous tasks that needed to be done in an age without machines. For instance, slaves provided the necessary labor for agriculture, building, and domestic chores. Their labor was an integral part of the economy. Slaves working in the fields had the least amount of protection and chances for freedom and were at best viewed as beasts of burden. Working on estates, they were subjected to beatings and forced to toil year-round. Comparable to field workers were those engaged in construction. These slaves did the dangerous tasks of working on roads, bridges, and buildings, with their lives often in danger from accidents. The domestic slaves had the most opportunity for manumission (freedom). They could be employed in the kitchens, in cleaning, in looking after children, and in other associated tasks. Domestic slaves were crucial in the functioning of the family. The household slaves were often the primary caregivers for the children. Their safety was not usually endangered, but they were more apt to be under the watchful eye of their masters. The worst lot for slaves happened to criminals assigned to the games or the mines. In either case their chances of surviving were slim.

CITIES, TOWNS, AND VILLAGES

Jewish families lived in a variety of settings. There were large cosmopolitan cities such as Rome, Athens, Corinth, Ephesus, Alexandria, and Caesarea. Large Jewish cities were few but included Jerusalem, the most important of all Jewish cities. More important were the smaller cities, villages, and towns throughout Palestine. For each of these areas there were differences that impacted the families.

Small villages and towns dotted the countryside throughout the ancient world. While these entities did not have a large population and often had only a few social classes, mainly peasants, they provided the local areas with a ready market and labor supply. Often the village housed the workers who cultivated the fields and provided the local market for buying and selling of agricultural goods. In addition to the agricultural workers, the village could also have some tradesmen, such as carpenters, blacksmiths, and stonemasons as well as muleteers and other transporters. The village was also the collection point for taxes and the dissemination of information by the government. The social structure of the village would have included mainly lower-class peasants, some middle-class merchants, shop owners, scribes, and religious officials, and perhaps an elite family. Not all villages would have upper-class families, but a village here or there might, especially if the family had seen their wealth increase over time and desired to remain in their ancestral home.

Larger villages or small towns would have been intermixed among the small villages and would have allowed for more specializations. For example, a village may not have had a carpenter because one lived in the small town nearby. The town would also act as a regional market where people from the small villages could get specialized materials or luxury items. These towns would have had more of a middle class and a governmental presence. The town would have had a more prominent religious function. In the New Testament period, towns would have had a synagogue that provided for the surrounding villages.

Unlike towns, which usually were constricted in size and amenities, cities provided the inhabitants and the surrounding area with more opportunities. These opportunities included expanded markets, variety of peoples and cultures, new and varied forms of entertainment, and increased social diffusion. In large Hellenistic cities, such as Caesarea, there were Greek components including theater, races, and pagan temples; there were Jewish elements such as synagogues and rabbinical schools; there were attributes of any large city such as trade organizations, shipping facilities, warehouses, and markets; and finally there were royal components: because Herod the Great had built this city as his capital, there was a palace that was later used by the Roman governor. This city attempted to allow the local Jewish and Greek population to live together in a cosmopolitan way. Unfortunately this did not always work out, because the two groups often were at odds with each other. There were occasional disputes, which spread into riots and violence. But these cities also allowed for the importation into the region of ideas, goods, and people from distant and different lands. This importation over time did alter the surrounding region, producing a different type of culture, different from the native Jewish and imported Greek. This new culture had elements of both and produced the synergy that was often a hallmark of antiquity.

In addition to cities that were cosmopolitan, the New Testament also had distinctively Jewish cities and towns. The most important was Jerusalem. Although the Greek monarchs from Syria during the Hellenistic period (300–150 B.C.E.) had attempted to import Greek ideas, the local Jewish population had resisted wholesale importation. Herod the Great's attempt to import Greek ideas, seen in the Fortress Antonia, had produced a negative backlash, because it was higher than his temple. Hellenistic culture faired even worse in the city, because Jerusalem was the religious capital of Judaism. The local Jewish political and religious authority, the high priest and Sanhedrin, were able to exert tremendous influence over the city. Roman governors usually did not reside in the city, because it was not Greek and they could not enjoy or enhance their normal public activities, especially the games. In addition, the Roman authorities could not carry out their pagan rituals, which underpinned the Roman state.

In the large cities the population was divided into social classes representing the social continuum. The majority of the inhabitants would have been the poor, which were divided into those who worked in the city and those who lived in the city but worked in the surrounding region. The city dwellers who worked in the city had a variety of occupations, from manual laborers to specialized functions. Moving up the social stratum were those engaged in trade. These would have included merchants, shop owners, money changers, and professionals. Finally at the top were the elites, which were likewise divided into different groups from those having new money to the traditional elites. The elites were able to control the financial and political life of the city. In return the elites provided stability and some protection for the city.

The city had numerous types of housing. There were the tenement houses where the great masses often lived. Although more common in Rome, tenements existed throughout the ancient world; typically they were multi-storied with numerous individual apartments having one or two rooms. There were single-family houses, which varied in size according to one's wealth. These homes, often multi-storied, could have courtyards with fountains and other ancillary buildings such as stables, storehouses, and workshops. Palatial structures existed in which numerous households lived together, providing not only the necessities of life but numerous other amenities.

In non-Jewish cities such as Caesarea, Ephesus, Athens, and Antioch, places visited by Paul and other early Christian missionaries during the first century C.E., Greek structures and life were common. Jews and later Christians made up only a small minority of the population, so the major emphasis showed the influence of Greek, Hellenistic, and Roman cultures. Baths, theaters, arenas, racetracks, and pagan temples were all hallmarks. In the mid-first century C.E., Herod Agrippa planned to announce his ascendancy in Palestine not in Jerusalem, but in the Greek-styled city of Caesarea where the non-Jewish population would support him. For Roman visitors the Greek cities were more comfortable than the Jewish cities such as Jerusalem.

With the destruction of Jerusalem and most of the countryside during the Great Jewish War and the war of the 130s C.E., the normal life of society and cities changed. Jerusalem was no longer just a Jewish city; in fact after 135 it became a Roman garrison city with a temple to Zeus on the site of Herod's Temple. Palestine became less Jewish in outlook and more like the regions of Syria and Asia Minor.

As the first century came to a close the Greek and Roman cities ultimately replaced the Jewish cities. This replacement further strengthened the move in daily life away from the Palestinian Jewish life toward the Greco-Roman culture. This shift ultimately led to the changes seen in the daily life away from rabbinical law and life toward a new law and life based on local influences and traditions.

BIOGRAPHY OF PAUL

Paul of Tarsus, born Saul, was born a Roman citizen in Tarsus Cilicia, the son of a Jew belonging to the tribe of Benjamin, knowing Greek and Aramaic. A Hellenized Jew, he allied himself with the Pharisees, having studied under Gamaliel. In the beginning he opposed Christianity and even helped in the martyrdom of Stephen. He approached the Jewish leaders, asking for permission to persecute the followers of Jesus in Damascus. Having received this commission he set out toward Damascus where, according to his account, he was struck blind by Jesus. Instructed to proceed to Damascus to find Ananias, he was cured and then baptized as a follower of Jesus. He went to Arabia for three years and then returned to Damascus before going to Jerusalem.

At Jerusalem he met and was accepted by Barnabas and was ultimately accepted by the other followers of Christ who initially doubted him. Traveling with Barnabas, Paul went to Cyprus, Barnabas's homeland, where he began his ministry. The two then traveled to Asia Minor into the interior, where they established churches at Antioch in Pisidia, Iconium, Lystra, and Derbe. They returned to Jerusalem, where the initial discussion of admission of the gentiles occurred. After the Apostles agreed to allow gentiles to be admitted as followers of Christ without circumcision, Paul traveled to Antioch, where the matter was fully decided. Paul and Barnabas separated, and Paul, with Timothy and Silas, traveled again through Asia Minor to Galatia and then to Greece. In Greece Paul established churches in Macedonia at Philippi, Thessalonica, and Berea. Meeting no success in Athens, Paul went to Corinth, where he established a successful church and met Aquila and Pricilla from Rome, who had been exiled by a decree of the Emperor Claudius exiling certain Jewish troublemakers (possibly Christians). He then traveled again to Asia Minor to Ephesus, where he composed his letters to the Corinthians, who were suffering from internal dissension.

After leaving Ephesus he returned to Jerusalem, where he was imprisoned by the corrupt procurator Felix who hoped to extort money from him and others. With the arrival of a new governor, Festus, Paul appealed to Caesar for a trial based on his Roman citizenship. After a harrowing sea voyage including a shipwreck at Malta, Paul arrived in Italy and was held in Rome under house arrest with a constant guard of Praetorian soldiers for two years. After a total of four or five years of imprisonment, Paul was released, possibly through a general amnesty by Nero. He may have traveled back to the East; there is only a late uncorroborated story of travel to Spain, before returning to Rome. He was arrested again, probably in connection with the fire and the general persecutions, and executed.

9

ROMAN OCCUPATION

Tell us, therefore, what do you think? Is it lawful to pay taxes to
Caesar, or not?...Show me the tax money. So they brought him
a *denarius*. And he said to them, Whose image and inscription
is this? They said to him, Caesar's. And he said to them render
therefore to Caesar the things that are Caesar's, and to God the
things that are God's. (Matt. 22:17–21)

ROME AND PALESTINE

Rome was drawn into Palestine and the region through a series of events
dating back to 179 B.C.E. During the height of the Republic Rome faced the
threat of Antiochus III of Syria and his attempt to take over Greece. Defeating Antiochus, Rome realized that other forces could be used to continuously chip away at Syrian power and influence. One of those forces was
the Jews, who had been clamoring for independence. Rome supported
this claim because it would destabilize Syria. Unfortunately for Rome, this
involvement would continually draw them into the internal problems of
Palestine.

After Herod the Great had died and been replaced by his son Archelaus, Rome became directly involved when the Jewish authorities asked
the Emperor Augustus to replace Archelaus. Although this helped solve
some of the internal and strategic problems it suddenly exposed a whole
set of new issues. Rome now became an occupier and with that came all of
the negative connotations.

The emperor ordered a census, a standard procedure for a new province, to determine not only the population but the economic strength of the province. This in turn led to riots and even violence. The census and its accompanying tax policies now pitted Rome against the local population. An example of how contentious an issue the tax policy was can be seen in the story in the New Testament in which Jesus is asked if it is acceptable to pay taxes to Caesar (Matt. 22:17–21). The attempt was to either have him say yes, in which case he would have been seen as an agent for Rome and would have lost all credibility with the Jewish populace, or have him say no, in which case he would have been seen by the Romans as a traitor. The payment or for that matter the avoidance of tax payments is important because it became a rallying point for both dissenters against and accommodators of the Romans. The Roman authorities consistently had problems with the Jewish populace over the payment of taxes.

CAESAREA

Unlike with most provinces, Rome had a precarious situation in Palestine during the New Testament time due to the religious peculiarities of monotheism. Unlike other provinces where Roman religion could meld with local religions, Palestine and Judaism resisted this interweaving. This also forced Rome to alter the normal practices of provincial government. As in all provinces, the Roman governor resided in the provincial capital. For many of the provinces it was the most important city. In Palestine the most important city was Jerusalem, but the capital was Herod the Great's Hellenistic city Caesarea. This city was Greek and on the coast, which allowed for a more cosmopolitan feel and one that looked outside of Palestine. For the governor, Caesarea allowed him to live in a Greek city with all of the amenities with which he was familiar and comfortable.

The city was a deep-water port, the only one in Palestine. The port had inner and outer harbors, allowing it to be an all-weather port as well. Using hydraulic cement, Herod, according to the historian Josephus, triumphed over nature. This claim was a bit exaggerated, because the outer harbor suffered from structural problems by the end of the first century C.E. Over the course of 12 years Herod refurbished the city, which included building an aqueduct, a palace, a hippodrome for horse/chariot races, and an amphitheater for gladiatorial contests. The palace stood on a promontory that extended into the sea, and it had a pool with stoas or covered walkways. The palace became the residence of the governor after the Romans took over. The population that grew to about 100,000 people, was equally distributed between Greeks and Jews, which often caused severe problems.

The Romans tended to prefer the Hellenistic cities rather than Jewish cities, even Jerusalem, which was a large multi-ethnic city. Jerusalem was a hotbed of trouble. Rome realized that a continual large presence of troops in the city would aggravate the situation usually based on religious differences. Roman governors for the most part were not understanding in Judea. They viewed themselves not only as the conquerors, but as the superiors in intellect, law, and culture. This superiority often led to arrogance.

Roman arrogance was well known. In the West, in Germany, this arrogance led to the military disasters of the governor Quintilius Varus in 9 C.E., who believed that after only 25 years the German tribes were "pacified." To Varus this meant that they were ready to accept Roman law and taxation. When Varus was attempting to enforce this pacification, he and his three legions were wiped out and Rome lost Germany. An interesting side note is that Varus had been governor of Syria and that he was known for his avaricious behavior in Palestine. In Britain this Roman arrogance led to the rebellion of the native tribes during Nero's reign under a local queen, Boudicca. The rebellion began when Rome nullified her husband's will, which gave joint power to Rome and to her; Roman officials seized the kingdom, beat her, and raped her daughters. This in turn led to rebellion.

In Palestine Rome seemingly was never able to get it right. From the start Roman policy tended to run counter to Jewish sentiment. For example, Rome placed on the throne Herod. While Herod was successful in buffering the East from Rome, his cruelty, even by the Emperor Augustus' standards, was extreme. After Herod's death his son Archelaus ruled so disastrously that Rome took over control. One of the first acts was the census, something forbidden in Jewish law, which led to rebellion. Any hope of good relations was now removed, in part because of Roman arrogance and Jewish customs. Both sides failed to understand the others. The Romans did not bother trying to determine what may or may not be allowed under Judaism, and the Jews failed to understand that Rome needed to account for the province. With this failure the two sides were now at constant odds.

The census takes an important role in the New Testament story. It is the vehicle by which Jesus' parents arrive at Bethlehem for his birth, fulfilling an ancient prophecy. But telling of the census is also an attempt to put Jesus within a historical event. Whether Joseph and Mary actually went to Bethlehem is not crucial; what is important is that the story would have resonated with everyone, Jew or gentile. The Romans were always conducting a census, and now Jesus was connected with a historical event, one that existed in nearly every province throughout the Roman world.

TAXES

Another area of Roman arrogance was in the collection of taxes. The exchange between Jesus and the Jewish authorities as to whether the Jews should pay taxes to Rome again highlights the issue. This issue does not mean that the Jews never paid taxes, or that they only paid taxes to Jewish rulers. After their defeat by Babylon in 586 B.C.E. the Jews remaining in Palestine must have paid taxes to Babylon. Even after their return in 537 B.C.E. they paid tolls and taxes to the Persian monarch on produce and consumption. After Alexander the Great the Jews paid taxes first to the Ptolemies, who farmed them out to the corporations who paid the highest amount upfront and then recouped the amount from the locals, while under the Syrians tribute was required, as well as a duty on salt, an agriculture tax, a poll tax, customs, and a tax of gold to the crown, the so-called *aurum coronarium,* which probably was given at the accession of a new king. During Herod's rule the tax was regularized into a property and income tax, sales tax, and import/export dues. He also imposed a tax on houses in Jerusalem.

Taxes, then, had existed for centuries in Palestine, and with the possible exception of Herod, had been levied by foreigners. But what made the Roman system so different? Roman taxation had a long history of being oppressive. This oppression may or may not have been real, but it was always seen as oppressive. During the Republic Roman, tax collectors were well known for enriching themselves. For example, in Sicily during the first century B.C.E. the Roman governor Verres allowed the tax collectors to exact such amounts that it nearly ruined the province. The great orator Cicero spoke against Verres, but the practice continued. What made the impression of oppression more real was that the Roman system, especially during the Empire, became more systematic. This regularization of the process made the taxes more predictable, but with predictability came a regular resentment. Further complementing this regularization was the continual centralization of the system. The Romans were excellent record-keepers and this allowed them to take full advantage of the resources in the provinces. While most of the money probably remained either in the province, or at least helped the province, the continual horror stories and anecdotes about tax money flowing to Rome for the pleasures of the emperor and his family only added to the resentment.

The tax system collected two main taxes, the capitation tax and the land tax. The capitation tax was levied on individuals at a constant rate, and for Palestine it seems to have been levied on both men and women over the age of 12, whether free or slave. The land tax was based on the agricultural capability of the region, usually one-tenth to one-twelfth of the grain produced, and one-fifth of the wine or fruit. The Romans usually collected the amounts in both material goods and money, depending upon the province. For example, in Egypt, Africa, and Sicily the tax was usually not paid in money but with produce, while in Greece the amounts were paid in money. In addition to these imperial taxes, there were charges paid on imports and exports transported on roadways and seaports. There exist some examples of the rates preserved on inscriptions. The commodities were of the usual types: clothing, food, and exotic goods, but they also

included slaves. In Judea what made the taxation onerous was that originally the tax money had ostensibly gone to the Temple for God, but now
it was going to Rome to the emperor.

But these reasons for hating taxation could have been applied to any
group that collected taxes in Judea. The Assyrians were well known for
their cruelty. The Persians and Babylonians collected taxes that went to
their gods and temples. The Ptolemies and Syrians imposed several different types of taxes. And Herod was known for being methodical in the
collection of taxes. So why did the Romans incur such hatred? Why did
the Jews continually see it differently than during the time of the Persians,
Ptolemies, or Syrians? One reason was cultural. Although Alexander the
Great and his successors were from the West, they had attempted to as-
similate and acculturate themselves in the Near Eastern environment. Alexander, Ptolemy, Seleucus, and the other Hellenistic kings adopted the
cultures of the Near East and their views of kingship. Although the Jews
opposed the concept of divine kings, it had existed elsewhere. Furthermore, with the exception of Antiochus IV and his cohorts, these rulers officially respected Jewish customs, even though local individuals and even
officials occasionally did not. The Romans, on the other hand, arrived and
proclaimed their superiority to the local inhabitants. Most importantly,
they did not attempt to learn about the region, seeing it only as an opportunity for enrichment. Pompey and his troops sacked Jerusalem, plunder-
ing the Temple. This act set the stage for future problems. Antony and
then Augustus placed Herod in charge, which further created distrust
and enmity toward Rome because of Herod's actions. The early governors after Herod did not understand the region; it was seen as merely
an opportunity for public advancement. This lack of sensitivity and the
Roman arrogance ensured that many in Palestine were upset. This anger
can be seen in the numerous attempts at rebellion and in the rise of the
Zealot party.

JEWISH-ROMAN LOCAL RELATIONS

Rome was not the only cause of problems. The local Jewish leadership
should also be blamed. Based on their petition after Herod Archelaus
that Rome take over, they ostensibly desired Rome, a non-Jewish entity,
to govern them. In many ways the local Jewish leadership wanted the
best of both worlds. They wanted protection, order, and help from a large
imperial government. They could also then state that they were against
this pagan, foreign, and arrogant police force, thus hoping to bring the
local population over to their side. By not doing the hard job of ruling,
and allowing another entity to rule, the Jews could declare that they were
merely being forced to do Rome's bidding. What the local leadership did
not indicate was how their own personal position was being enriched at
the expense of the local population.

Neither side, however, wanted the other to succeed within the framework of the eastern Mediterranean. Rome feared that any form of independence would be an opening for their arch-enemy, the Parthians, to attack, something that had happened the previous century; the Jews feared that any cooperation with Rome might lead to a loss of religious identity. The end result was that Rome and the population were constantly at odds with one another, ready for a flare-up.

This flare-up was constant. Any time Roman governors made a mistake, and there were plenty, the locals, often encouraged by the local Jewish leadership, protested, often violently. The procurator (governor) Pontius Pilate is perhaps best known. According to Josephus, Pilate had the legionary standards brought into Jerusalem at night. Being discovered, the Jews protested and for five days Pilate ignored them. He finally allowed them in for an audience and threatened to kill them if they did not desist. According to Josephus, the Jews bared their necks, declaring they would rather die than see an outrage committed. Pilate then relented and removed the standards. Another time, according to the historian Philo, he had golden shields erected in the fortress in Jerusalem with the name of the Emperor Tiberius. When the Jews found out they demanded their removal, which he refused. They in turn appealed to the Tiberius, who ordered them to be removed and sent to Caesarea. For Pilate this would have been a no-win situation, once he erected them. If he gave in to the demands he would have been insulting the emperor; by not giving in he ended up insulting the Jews. Of course he should not have done it in the first place. Another mistake was using Temple money to build an aqueduct for the city of Jerusalem. While no one would object to clean fresh water, how it was paid for created an issue, one not solved peacefully. After it became known that Temple money was used, a bloody riot took place, which was only squashed by the soldiers. The Jews were just as troublesome for the Romans. Their refusal to allow the Romans and non-Jews to worship their gods in Jerusalem seemed outrageous to Rome. Their argument that they should not pay taxes to the emperor but demanded the Romans pay taxes to their God, which the Romans did as a contribution, seemed to be hypocritical. Finally, continual insistence on refusing to honor the emperor when everyone else did struck the Romans as mere stubbornness.

What is important to understand is not that the actions of either group were correct or incorrect, but rather that both groups seemingly did not want to communicate. Although it is true that Rome was the occupier, it should be remembered that throughout their early relationship, the Romans were called in for help. Although the Jews had a different idea of what this help entailed, wanting Rome to give them aid and then leave, Rome responded with aid, and the expectation that they could stay or at least influence the region. This continual struggle is what ultimately led to the great wars in 66–73 and 132–135 C.E.

BEYOND PALESTINE

Outside of Palestine the situation was a bit different. While locals always viewed Rome as oppressive, occupiers, and indifferent, the level of discontent did not usually rise to rebellion. In Asia Minor Rome had replaced the Hellenistic leaders who, like the Persian before, had continually collected taxes and controlled local communities. Rome now merely supplanted the top ruler while at the same time giving back to the local regions in the form of protection, communication, and economic development. During the first century B.C.E. the region was beset with security problems. The king of Bithynia in the north, Mitridates, had attacked the western and southern parts of Asia Minor, causing turmoil. This was followed by the rise of pirates on the coastline of Asia Minor, commonly referred as the Cilician Pirates (named for one of the regions, Cilicia). These pirates intercepted merchant ships, which threatened grain supplies throughout the Mediterranean. Rome ultimately intervened, and Pompey successfully dealt with both Mitridates and the pirates. With the arrival of Rome and its military, new roads and seaports were developed. These activities allowed for an ease of communication. This in turn, together with the increased security, allowed for economic development. This development is best seen in the rise of long-distance trade. Merchants were now able to trade not only in peace but across long distances, because the Romans created a system in which trade barriers were no longer in place. During the Hellenistic period, the local kingdoms effectively prevented certain trade opportunities from occurring by imposing high tariffs and other impediments. With Rome these impediments were removed and the Mediterranean became safer, allowing for an increase in trade.

The local regions continued in their attempt to retain their identities. This is best seen in art. According to popular belief, Roman culture reached its height during the early imperial age. Early imperial Roman culture (14–235 C.E.), mainly the plastic arts of statues, sculptural relief, and paintings, attempted to distinguish itself from the earlier republican period or Eastern Hellenism, especially in the provinces. Such a process is called Romanization, defined as the merging of Roman, and, in essence, Hellenistic culture, with local customs, crafts, and themes, or the fusion of the Classical world with non-Classical regions. Although in Palestine it did not take place as readily as elsewhere, there was nevertheless an attempt by Herod to make this fusion in his palaces at Caesarea, Masada, and other non-Jewish sites.

Romanization occurred most profoundly in the West, because the East exported Hellenism to Rome during the late Republic. The Romans then exported their culture into the West, where they fused it with local cultures, such as the Gallic religion or Punic (African) architecture. In the East this fusion did exist but not to the same extent as in the West. During the early Empire it is clear that Rome, that is, Italy, took the lead in the practice of Romanization, with the local elites following closely behind to integrate themselves with the Romans and maintain or obtain power; many regions received Roman culture unwillingly, as a form of cultural imperialism. Roman soldiers, bureaucrats, and colonists arrived in newly conquered Western "barbarian" lands, bringing with them Roman-Italian culture, building Roman administrative cities and villas, and imposing Roman cultural ideas on the indigenous populations. As a means of social, economic, and political advancement, local elites adopted and imitated Roman culture. Finally, this adoption produced a local hybridization of Roman themes, crafts, and customs melded with the native ones, producing Romanization.

The impact this had on society and daily life should not be ignored. For the local population in Palestine the constant barrage of Roman, that is, pagan, motifs often must have been seen as an attempt to swamp the local region, and this barrage came not only from the Roman overseers but from the local leadership as well. Starting with Herod and his family and then accelerated by local Jewish leaders, the influx of Hellenism or Roman ideology must have been awkward or confusing for the locals. The ultimate response was a conflict between Roman and Jewish ideas. The conflict ultimately destroyed the Jewish way of life in Palestine at the end of the New Testament time and completed the split between Judaism and Christianity.

For the lives of the people in Palestine, society had seen tremendous upheavals during the late first century C.E. The local population would continue to live as they had done before, toiling in the fields, trying to make ends meet, and always being forced to pay more taxes; but their connection with the old religious life would be gone. With the destruction of Palestine and the failure of a revived Jewish state, the political world was now Roman, while the religious world was fragmented.

BIOGRAPHIES OF AUGUSTUS AND HEROD

Augustus

Born Gaius Octavius (63 B.C.E.–14 C.E.), he changed his name to Gaius Julius Caesar after Julius Caesar's assassination and adoption (in his will), but he is better known as Augustus, the name given to him in 27 B.C.E. by the Roman Senate. His mother, a niece of Julius Caesar, raised him after his father's death in 58 B.C.E., and Julius Caesar promoted him into public life, having Octavius accompany him to Spain in 45 and sending him to Apollonia in Epirus to complete his studies, where he was residing when Caesar was assassinated in 44 B.C.E. Returning to Italy to claim his inheritance, both monetary and political, Octavius first battled Mark Antony and then joined him to combat the murderers of Caesar, Brutus and Cassius. He joined with

Antony and Marcus Lepidus to create to Second Triumvirate (rule of three). When Julius Caesar was declared a god the next year, 42 B.C.E., Octavius became, in effect, the son of a god due to his being the adopted son of Caesar. The Triumvirate then defeated Brutus and Cassius at Philippi in Macedonia. Octavius married Scribonia, a relative of Sextus Pompey, who had rallied senators opposed to Julius Caesar and the subsequent Triumvirate to Sicily. Sextus Pompey had begun to terrorize the grain ships heading to Rome. The marriage was an attempt to bring about a truce, one that was only temporary. The marriage produced Octavian's only child, a daughter Julia. Divorcing Scribonia in 40 B.C.E., he married Livia Drusilla, who would remain his wife till his death.

Antony had married Octavius's sister Octavia. However, in the East Antony had become enamored with Cleopatra and abandoned Octavia, with whom he had two daughters, Antonia Major and Antonia Minor. Octavius's general, Agrippa, successfully defeated Sextus Pompey and removed Lepidus from power. Antony remained opposed to Octavius. In 31 B.C.E. the two met at Actium, and Agrippa, leading Octavius's fleet, routed Antony, who now fled to Egypt with Cleopatra, where they committed suicide the following year when Octavius arrived. Seizing Egypt and its resources, Octavius demobilized a sizable number of troops, giving them land and money as rewards. Upon returning to Italy, Octavius now made a series of political settlements that guaranteed his power. He held the power of tribunes, giving him the right to veto any act and to introduce legislation, the power of a consul, giving him the power to command the armies, and the financial resources of the empire. In 27 B.C.E. he became known as Augustus, signifying his saving the Roman state.

During this time Augustus began the process of planning his succession. He married his only child, a daughter Julia, to his nephew Marcellus. After Marcellus's death in 23 B.C.E., Augustus gave her in marriage to his general Agrippa. Because Agrippa was only an equites, therefore unsuitable in the Senate's eyes to succeed the emperor, Augustus adopted Agrippa and Julia's sons Gaius and Lucius as his own sons. Agrippa died in 12 B.C.E. and Augustus now forced Julia to marry Tiberius, his stepson, who had to divorce his wife. This marriage was not happy and soon Julia was accused of adultery and banished to a small island. Augustus blamed Tiberius, who went into forced exile. With the death of Gaius and Lucius, however, Tiberius was recalled because he was the only individual of age and competence whom Augustus could rely on. Augustus died in 14 C.E.

Herod

Herod the Great, born in 73 B.C.E. in Idumea, was the son of Antipater and Cyprus, a daughter of an Arabian sheik. Antipater supported the Jewish king Hyrcanus, and both supported Julius Caesar in the civil war. Antipater secured for his 16-year-old son Herod the governorship of Galilee, after which he waged a campaign against bandits. He was condemned by the Sanhedrin for his brutal actions in Galilee. After the death of Julius Caesar, the ensuing struggle between his murderers and Octavius and Antony, nephew and second-in-command respectively, resulted in chaos in the East. Antipater was murdered and Herod now avenged him. Herod then married into the Jewish royal family by taking Mariamne as his wife. This in turn allowed him to be closely in line to the throne.

Antony made Herod ruler of Galilee and Herod's brother ruler of Jerusalem. The Jews viewed Herod as an outsider, because his family was only recently converted to Judaism. Herod ultimately was made king of Judea by the Romans in 37 B.C.E. Herod's rule was based upon the concept of maintaining good relations with Rome and the Jewish religious leaders. In foreign policy he had difficult relations with Cleopatra of Egypt but maintained good relations with Mark Antony. With the defeat of Antony by Octavian, Herod executed the last king, Hyrcanus, and then met Octavian and reconciled with him.

The most enduring accomplishment of Herod's rule was the building program he undertook. He built a new city, Caesarea Maritime, in the style of a Greek city. In Jerusalem he built a series of new buildings, an amphitheater, market, fortress (Antonia), and palace. His greatest achievement, started in 20 B.C.E., was the Temple. Herod did not win the hearts of his subjects. He upset the Sadducees when he eliminated the old royal house that they were aligned with. The Pharisees disliked him because he went against the Jewish laws. He introduced new taxes that were unpopular.

He had an unhappy family life, seeing conspiracies and enemies everywhere. He executed several of his wives and sons. He died of a horrible disease, possibly chronic kidney disease and Fournier's gangrene. Known for his brutality, Herod successfully maintained his power through fear and intimidation. His successors were not as politically apt as Herod, and Rome ultimately stepped in and occupied Judea.

10

CONCLUSION

Daily life during the first century C.E. was directly influenced by religion and in turn influenced the religious evolution of Judaism and later Christianity. In Palestine Judaism maintained many of its tenets even though the region had been overrun and controlled by pagan societies. Although they had won the political battle against the Seleucid kingdom under the Maccabees, they had in many ways lost the cultural war against Hellenism. During their independence and then their semi-autonomous rule under Herod the Great, Judaism maintained much of its religious identity. This identity was saved mainly by the Pharisees, who were uncompromising in the religious struggle between Hellenism and Judaism while they tolerated foreign control. But the Pharisees were unable to convince many of the newly won areas, such as Galilee, that their political philosophy of waiting for the Messiah and tolerating Roman rule should be followed. Into this mix entered Jesus. During his early life there had been a rebellion by a local Galilean over the census. Later his kinsman, John, was executed by Herod Antipas for condemning his marriage to his brother's ex-wife. Jesus was likewise potentially at risk and in fact had to flee Galilee to avoid problems. Jesus was constantly preaching against many of the problems facing the Jews in Palestine. For example, he preached against the harsh rules imposed by the Pharisees and Sadducees. He preached against the recent innovation of divorce and remarriage, which the Pharisees had accepted. He argued for the concept of the resurrection, which the Sadducees had been fighting. Finally, he advocated that he was the Messiah without detailing what type of Messiah. All of this happened within a backdrop of the political realities, Palestine being a region occupied by the Roman Empire. This occupation led to a rebellion and the destruction of Jerusalem in 70 c.e.

The destruction of Jerusalem and the occupation of Judea by the Romans secured the cultural victory of Hellenism over Judaism in the first century c.e. The end of Judaism as a political entity, which had been backed by the Zealots and Sadducees, ensured the victory of Hellenism over Judaism in the eastern Mediterranean. Although this did not mean that Judaism converted to Hellenism in all of its form, it did mean that the region of Palestine was no longer exclusively Jewish. In addition, this defeat of Judaism as a culture changed how society viewed itself, namely the divisions that existed. The Zealots, Essenes, and Sadducees were gone; the Pharisees emerged as the only remnant of the old political-religious parties. The Pharisees survived because they had already adapted through the use of the synagogues.

Because Jesus preached his message to the Jews and followed the main ideas of the Pharisees, it is best to view them originally as a sect of the Pharisees. Therefore we can say the one group of Pharisees was the Christians, the followers of Jesus. The similarities between the two were profound and their differences, although major in Christians viewing Jesus as the Messiah, were not that great. The rebellion, however, provided a final break between the two, one that had already begun with Paul's missionary activities into Asia Minor, Greece, and Italy, where he attempted to convert not only Jews but gentiles. The early Christian Jews, best seen in James, the apostle of Jesus and leader in Jerusalem, were Pharisees. Previously Judaism and Christianity, being part of the same religion, followed the Jewish customs, most noticeably the dietary laws. In early Christianity many of Jesus' disciples were from the Pharisees. James, the bishop of Jerusalem, appears to have been an ardent supporter of the Pharisees. His interactions and views reflected those of mainstream Judaism, the Pharisees, and often brought him into conflict with more liberal elements of Christian Jews.

The best example was the debate over circumcision. While James argued that followers of Jesus should first undergo circumcision, thereby becoming Jews, Paul, a fellow Pharisee, argued against it. Paul's view became the accepted mode, meaning that converts did not have to become Jewish. This debate can be seen not only as a religious discussion, but a cultural one as well (Acts 15:1–15). Those who followed James, the Jewish Christians, aligned themselves with the Jewish cultural practices, while those who supported Paul, the gentile Christians, were more apt to follow Hellenistic ideals. But with the rebellion many of the Christians, especially the gentiles, desired to separate themselves from the political wars and show their loyalty to or at least their noncombative stance with Rome. What the defeat in Judea allowed was for Christianity to break away from Judaism and set out on its own course. Combining with Hellenism through philosophy, Christianity became even more acceptable to the gentiles. This change resulted in a different way of life.

With the separation of Christianity from Judaism a whole slew of dietary laws were no longer enforced. The change meant that gentiles did not have to give up their current practices regarding types and preparation of food. For example, in many of the Greek areas the eating of pork was allowed; with the split, gentile Christians could continue to eat an animal that Jews had found unclean. These changes in turn allowed Christianity to spread beyond the local Jewish population. The number of gentile Christians soon outnumbered the Jewish Christians, which further reduced the power and influence of the old Pharisee sect. With the removal of forced circumcision, gentiles now found the ideas of monotheism and Christianity more appealing and easier to accept. The rise of Christianity among the gentiles and the diminishing role of Christian Jews resulted in outward changes in rituals. For example, the traditional worship days changed. Originally Jews worshiped on Mondays and Thursdays, but Christians now moved this to Wednesdays and Fridays. The Jewish Sabbath was now replaced with the Christian Sunday. These changes by the Christians were instituted for the purpose of making the differences between Judaism and Christianity more recognizable. While it is difficult to know precisely how the changes took place, it is clear that within a century Christianity outnumbered Judaism, in part due to its ease of spread. Individuals no longer needed to worship and follow the strict Jewish customs.

The impact of daily life during New Testament times on modern society is not necessarily obvious. But if one were to examine the rituals and obligations of Christians during the medieval centuries there would have been immense similarities. Worship would still have been stressed for certain days of the week, especially Wednesdays and Fridays. Fasting on these days was likewise constantly observed. Abstinence from meat on Fridays was practiced. And the celebration of the religious seasons that led up to the great Jewish and now Christian festivals of Passover and Pentecost were readily apparent.

The transference of Jewish ideology in art could be been seen in the Eastern churches and the struggles that erupted over the icons. During the ninth century C.E. there was a movement in the Byzantine state and Church to outlaw the use of the icons. The basis of this attack on the icons stemmed from the interpretation by a segment of Christianity that icons were seen as idols. This idea, rooted in Jewish ideology, ripped the Eastern Church apart for nearly a century. Although the issue was ultimately decided in favor of keeping the adoration of the icons, the underlying view of icons being seen as idols persisted.

The biggest impact that occurred was in the area of theology and religious change. The Jewish belief system of monotheism, originally viewed during the first century C.E. as alien and superstitious, was now made available to a wider audience through the fusion of Judaism and Hellenistic philosophy. This fusion now allowed the concept of monotheism, with the idea of Jesus as the Messiah, to be infused into Greco-Roman society. Although at first seen as barbaric and alien, it was ultimately accepted as the official state religion within three centuries. This new theology of Judaism, Jesus as the Messiah, and Greek philosophy produced in its final form the theology of Augustine, who argued that Christianity was not the reason why the Roman Empire was beset by problems; rather, it would be why Rome would be saved. In his works, *City of God* and *Confessions,* Augustine would lay out not only his own transformation but the ideas that would allow Christianity to flourish. His philosophy and theology were not only grounded in Greek rhetoric but in the knowledge of the Old Testament. The impact of this philosophy and theology continues to this day.

The change in religion is the greatest impact today. The growth of Christianity from a sect of Judaic Pharisees to a major religion must be counted as one of the greatest phenomena of history. The expansion of Christianity began in Palestine and spread through Asia Minor. The growth was not through simple diffusion, spreading from one point to the next; rather it spread from one city to another by hopping over regions. For example, the spread of Christianity did not go from Antioch and then to the next city; rather it spread to Cyprus and then to the mainland. Cities such as Ephesus, Pergamum, Smyrna, and the region of Galatia received Christianity while other regions in between did not accept or even receive missionaries. This spread into gentile regions soon accelerated and spread to Greece, to cities such as Philippi, Thessalonica, and Corinth. After spreading to these major cities Christianity then followed two routes; first there was a movement to expand Christianity to the West, and second to backfill the areas in the East. The first saw Christianity introduced into Italy and North Africa. Following the same diffusion system as in the East, Christianity spread to the major cities before jumping off to new regions such as Spain and Gaul and then backfilling the regions of Africa and Italy. By the end of the second century C.E. Christianity had become entrenched in Asia Minor, Greece, Egypt, North Africa, and Italy. Throughout the third century the new religion spread to the Rhine and Danube region and into the hinterland of Spain. By the end of the third century, when Diocletian enacted his last persecution to rid the empire of this alien religion, it was too late. By 337 C.E. when Constantine died, Christianity was well on its way to becoming the predominant religion and the official state religion by 391 C.E. under Theodosius.

This religious growth developed separately and outside of Palestine and Judaism. When the rebellions of the 60s and 130 failed to establish an independent Jewish state, there was no hope that Christianity would reunite with Judaism. Palestine was now a changed land as well. The wars caused tremendous upheavals that would impact the future. The destruction of the Temple, which some hoped would be rebuilt, ultimately led to the end of a major, albeit small, faction of Judaism, the Sadducees. This group, which claimed its power based on the Temple, was now unable to survive. A second group, the Essenes, likewise became extinct. This group, however, has influenced modern society through its archaeological remains, including the Dead Sea Scrolls.

The Dead Sea Scrolls provide an important link between the first century C.E. and the twenty-first century. Although the scrolls tell us little about their daily life, they do inform us about some aspects of society, religion, and politics. In addition to the scrolls, there were other finds that help us understand society at this time. The scrolls were found with linen cloths. It appears that the linen cloths were used to wrap the scrolls, probably for protection. Some of the linen material may have been used for regular clothing for individuals. Coins were discovered at the site, including three ceramic containers filled with silver coins. It is possible that these vessels represented the worldly possessions of new initiates who had to surrender their worldly goods, or it may have been an accumulation of the sect's possessions put under the doorway for safety. The fact that it was not recovered until the twentieth century attests to the ability of some to hide their goods. Over 1,000 pieces of pottery, mainly of utilitarian use, have been discovered at the site. Most were used for daily dining use, including plates, jugs, cups, and bowls. These remains indicate that the site was used as a residential community and that there seems not to have been a separation of classes in which one had luxurious items and others mad do with common goods. This probably indicates that the site was indeed a community rather than a villa.

Located in the ruins of the Essene community at Qumran was a large number of pottery remains, including in one building that had over a thousand vessels arranged by function. Some of the scrolls themselves were found in pottery vessels. The use of pottery vessels allowed the material to remain dry and protected. Discovered materials included plates, jugs, lamps, and cups, all used in everyday life. Some of them were even stacked as if in a modern kitchen cupboard. In and around the site were discovered leather goods, mainly made of sheepskin, used for water skins, purses, garments, and sandals. Some woodwork has been recovered from Qumran, including bowls and combs. The combs are made of boxwood and are double-sided, a familiar type in antiquity. The site also had phylactery cases that contained small chambers to hold small pieces of paper for prayers. The sizes of these cases were small, only 1 inch by 1/2 inch, and were meant to be fastened to one's clothes. Several phylacteries have been found. The phylactery would contain two verses from the book of Deuteronomy (6:4–9; 11:13–21) and two from Exodus (13:1–10; 13:11–16). Stone vessels, unlike pottery, which when used became ritually unclean and needed to be broken so as not to be used again, could be used repeatedly and did not become ritually unclean. The remains of these stone vessels, not only in Qumran but in Jerusalem and elsewhere, attest to their need and common use. Measuring cups, storage vessels, and drinking cups made of limestone were all discovered; their

Area surrounding the Dead Sea (Bahr Lut). The Ancient fortress of Masada (Seb-
beh). Courtesy of Library of Congress.

use in Palestine came to an end with the destruction of the Temple in 70 C.E.
These finds indicate that the community used material that was commonly
found throughout Palestine.

The scrolls contain fragments of every book of the Old Testament except
the book of Esther. This is important because it shows how the evolution
of the Old Testament was an ongoing process. Although the texts are fragmentary, they are nevertheless authoritative, that is, they correspond to the
text as it has come down through the centuries. The scrolls also attest to
the idea that local synagogues during Jesus' time would have books of the
Bible. In one passage Jesus opens and reads from the work of Isaiah (Luke
4:16–22), presumably on a scroll like that found in Qumran. The fragments
found are in three languages, Hebrew, Aramaic, and Greek. This again attests to the cosmopolitan linguistic feature of the region and time in which
Jesus and his followers lived. The scrolls contain material not found in
the Bible, but that is religious in nature. For example, there is a scroll that
contains both Psalms that are in the Bible and others that are not. In addition to these religious texts, there are also scrolls that cover community
life, and a calendar scroll showing that the community followed the solar
year of 364 days and not the traditional Jewish lunar calendar of 354 days.

Roman encampment from Masada. Courtesy of Library of Congress.

According to this calendar the New Year always started on a Wednesday, the day God created the heavens.

The scrolls provide a look at a community, which had separated itself from mainstream Judaism. Although known from Josephus's work, the community remained a complete mystery until the discovery of the scrolls in 1947. Since that time their history has unfolded, slowly and not without controversy. The scrolls and their discovery point to another aspect of studying daily life during the New Testament period, and that is that new discoveries are occurring. Recently a quarry dating from the time of Herod the Great was unearthed in Jerusalem and points to its use for the construction of the Temple. South of the Dead Sea the fortress of Masada has been excavated, yielding new pieces of data that help us understand Josephus's account. The archaeological remains continue to provide scholars with opportunities to question and explore the first century in the modern age. The siege of Masada has invoked admiration for the defenders and debate as to the validity of Josephus's account of the mass suicide. Regardless of its validity, it stands as a testament to the image of the Jews defiant until death in preserving their religion and their way of life.

JOSEPHUS'S ACCOUNT OF THE MASS SUICIDE
AT THE SIEGE OF MASADA

How the People That Were in the Fortress Were Prevailed on by the Words of
Eleazar, Two Women and Five Children Only Excepted and All Submitted
to Be Killed by One Another

1. NOW as Eleazar was proceeding on in this exhortation, they all cut him off short, and made haste to do the work, as full of an unconquerable ardor of mind, and moved with a demoniacal fury. So they went their ways, as one still endeavoring to be before another, and as thinking that this eagerness would be a demonstration of their courage and good conduct, if they could avoid appearing in the last class: so great was the zeal they were in to slay their wives and children, and themselves also! Nor indeed, when they came to the work itself, did their courage fail them, as one might imagine it would have done; but they then held fast the same resolution, without wavering, which they had upon the hearing of Eleazar's speech, while yet every one of them still retained the natural passion of love to themselves and their families, because the reasoning they went upon appeared to them to be very just, even with regard to those that were dearest to them; for the husbands tenderly embraced their wives, and took their children into their arms, and gave the longest parting kisses to them, with tears in their eyes. Yet at the same time did they complete what they had resolved on, as if they had been executed by the hands of strangers, and they had nothing else for their comfort but the necessity they were in of doing this execution, to avoid that prospect they had of the miseries they were to suffer from their enemies. Nor was there at length any one of these men found that scrupled to act their part in this terrible execution, but every one of them dispatched his dearest relations. Miserable men indeed were they! whose distress forced them to slay their own wives and children with their own hands, as the lightest of those evils that were before them. So they being not able to bear the grief they were under for what they had done, any longer, and esteeming it an injury to those they had slain, to live even the shortest space of time after them; they presently laid all they had upon a heap, and set fire to it. They then chose ten men by lot out of them to slay all the rest; every one of whom laid himself down by his wife and children on the ground, and threw his arms about them, and they offered their necks to the stroke of those who by lot executed that melancholy office; and when these ten had, without fear, slain them all, they made the same rule for casting lots for themselves, that he whose lot it was should first kill the other nine, and after all should kill himself. Accordingly, all these had courage sufficient to be no way behind one another in doing or suffering; so, for a conclusion, the nine offered their necks to the executioner, and he who was the last of all took a view of all the other bodies, lest perchance some or other among so many that were slain should want his assistance to be quite dispatched, and when he perceived that they were all slain, he set fire to the palace, and with the great force of his hand ran his sword entirely through himself, and fell down dead

near to his own relations. So these people died with this intention, that they would not leave so much as one soul among them all alive to be subject to the Romans. Yet was there an ancient woman, and another who was of kin to Eleazar, and superior to most women in prudence and learning, with five children, who had concealed themselves in caverns underground, and had carried water thither for their drink, and were hidden there when the rest were intent upon the slaughter of one another. Those others were nine hundred and sixty in number, the women and children being withal included in that computation. This calamitous slaughter was made on the fifteenth day of the month Xanthicus [Nisan].

2. Now for the Romans, they expected that they should be fought in the morning, when accordingly, they put on their armour, and laid bridges of planks upon their ladders from their banks, to make an assault upon the fortress, which they did; but saw nobody as an enemy, but a terrible solitude on every side, with a fire within the place, as well as a perfect silence. So they were at a loss to guess at what had happened. At length they made a shout, as if it had been at a blow given by the battering ram, to try whether they could bring any one out that was within; the women heard this noise, and came out of their under-ground cavern, and informed the Romans what had been done, as it was done; and the second of them clearly described all both what was said and what was done, and this manner of it; yet did they not easily give their attention to such a desperate undertaking, and did not believe it could be as they said; they also attempted to put the fire out, and quickly cutting themselves a way through it, they came within the palace, and so met with the multitude of the slain, but could take no pleasure in the fact, though it were done to their enemies. Nor could they do other than wonder at the courage of their resolution, and the immovable contempt of death which so great a number of them had shown, when they went through with such an action as that was.

Source: The Works of Josephus, trans. William Whiston (William Milner Cheapside, 1850), pp. 628–29.

GLOSSARY

Diaspora: refers to the Jews who were forced to leave Palestine after the Babylonians captured Jerusalem.

Essenes: religious group during the first century that separated themselves from mainstream Judaism and believed that the Sadducees were corrupt.

Gnostic: meaning knowledge, referred to writings in which the secret message had to be understood from within rather than through the mediation of the Church.

Gospels: meaning good news, can refer to the four canonical texts in the New Testament, Matthew, Mark, Luke, and John, or the noncanonical texts, usually Gnostic works, that purported to reveal the hidden truths of Jesus.

Hasmonaean: ruling dynasty in Palestine from 140–37 B.C.E.

Herodians: the political party that supported Herod the Great and his successors. They were generally pro-Roman.

Kohen: Hebrew word for priest.

Koine **Greek:** meaning common Greek, developed after Alexander the Great that became the standard Greek, both written and oral, during the time of Jesus.

Korban: the Temple sacrifice dedicated by the priests.

Messiah: literally, anointed one; referred to in Judaism as the expected savior. The Messiah was never clearly defined but was to be descended from David, king of Israel.

New Testament: means the New Covenant or agreement between God and the Christians, fulfilled in Jesus; the part of the Bible that tells of the origins of Christianity.

Pentateuch: Greek term that refers to the first five books of Old Testament, in Hebrew the Torah.

Pharisee: meaning separated, the predominant group in Judaism during the first century C.E. They developed outside of the Temple complex and after the destruction of Jerusalem became the rabbinic party.

Publicans: tax collectors employed by Rome. Usually they were native inhabitants.

Qumran: a site on the northwest shore of the Dead Sea where archaeological remains indicate that the Essenes had their community. Nearby the Dead Sea Scrolls were discovered in caves beginning in 1947.

Sabbath: a weekly day of worship in which no work was to be performed. In Judaism it falls on Saturday, in Christianity, Sunday.

Sadducee: developed in the second century B.C.E., they were the ruling party, both politically and later through the Temple. Although not numerous, they held the highest political offices.

Samaria: region north of Judea that was occupied by the Samaritans, who although offshoots of the Jews, believed that they held the traditional site of the Temple.

Sanhedrin: meaning assembly, was a body of 23 elders or judges that decided policies. In Jerusalem, the Great Sanhedrin, a body of 71, decided policies relating not only to Jerusalem but concerning the Temple.

Scribes: the lawyers in Judaism.

Sicarii: meaning dagger men, referred to the assassins who attacked Romans and pro-Roman inhabitants of Palestine.

Synagogue: a house of prayer or assembly; developed after the Babylonian Exile and became the predominant house of study or worship during the New Testament period.

Talmud: rabbinic works or teachings that relate to Jewish laws, customs, history, and ethics. The two components were the oral traditions, the Mishnah (reduced to writing in 200 C.E.) and the Gemara, which were originally oral commentaries on the Mishnah. There exist the Babylonian Talmud and the Jerusalem Talmud.

Targum: an Aramaic translation and commentary on the Old Testament, probably used in the synagogues throughout Palestine.

Temple: refers here to the structure in Jerusalem completed by Herod the Great and used for worship during the time of Jesus, destroyed in 70 C.E. by the Romans.

Zealots: religious group in Palestine that believed in the violent overthrow of the Roman occupation of Palestine.

BIBLIOGRAPHY

Aviam, Mordechai. *Jews, Pagans, and Christians in the Galilee, 25 Years of Archaeological Excavations and Surveys: Hellenistic to Byzantine Periods*. Land of Galilee, vol. 1. Rochester, NY: University of Rochester Press, 2004.

Beall, Todd S. *Josephus' Description of the Essenes Illustrated by the Dead Sea Scrolls*. Cambridge: Cambridge University Press, 2004.

Beyer, Klaus. *The Aramaic Language: Its Distribution and Subdivisions*, trans. John F. Healey. Gottingen: Vandenhoeck and Ruprecht, 1986.

Borowski, Oded. *Daily Life in Biblical Times. Archaeology and Biblical Studies*. Vol. 5. Atlanta, GA: Society of Biblical Literature, 2003.

Burrows, Millar. *The Dead Sea Scrolls with Translation by the Author*. New York: Viking, 1956.

Case, Shirley Jackson. *The Historicity of Jesus*. University of Chicago Press, 1912.

Chilton, Bruce, and Jacob Neusner. *The Brother of Jesus: James the Just and His Mission*. Louisville, KY: Westminster John Knox Press, 2001.

Fine, Steven. *Art and Judaism in the Greco-Roman World toward a New Jewish Archaeology*. Cambridge: Cambridge University Press, 2005.

———. "Synagogues in the Land of Israel." In *Near Eastern Archaeology: A Reader*, ed. Suzanne Richard, pp. 455–64. Winona Lake, IN: Eisenbrauns, 2003.

Fosdick, Harry. *The Man from Nazareth*. New York: Harper and Brothers, 1949.

Gilen, Terry. "The Samaritans." In *Near Eastern Archaeology: A Reader*, ed. Suzanne Richard, pp. 413–17. Winona Lake, IN: Eisenbrauns, 2003.

Goodman, Martin. *Jews in a Graeco-Roman World*. Oxford: Clarendon Press, 1998.

Grant, Michael. *The Ancient Mediterranean*. New York: Penguin, 1969.

———. *Cleopatra*. New York: Barnes and Noble Books, 1995.

———. *The History of Ancient Israel*. London: Weidenfeld and Nicolson, 1996.

Hachlili, Rachel. "Jewish Art and Iconography in the Land of Israel." In *Near East-
    ern Archaeology: A Reader,* ed. Suzanne Richard, pp. 445–54. Winona Lake,
    IN: Eisenbrauns, 2003.
Harland, Philip A. *Associations, Synagogues, and Congregations Claiming a Place in
    Ancient Mediterranean Society.* Minneapolis, MN: Fortress Press, 2003.
Hetzron, Robert, ed. *The Semitic Languages.* London: Routledge, 1997.
Hoehner, Harold W. *Herod Antipas.* Cambridge: Cambridge University Press, 1972.
Hopkins, David. "Agriculture." In *Near Eastern Archaeology: A Reader,* ed. Suzanne
    Richard, pp. 124–30. Winona Lake, IN: Eisenbrauns, 2003.
Huntington, Ellsworth. *The Climate of Ancient Palestine.* New York, 1908.
Jeffers, James S. *The Greco-Roman World of the New Testament Era: Exploring the Back-
    ground of Early Christianity.* Downers Grove, IL: InterVarsity Press, 1999.
Josephus, Flavius. *Life of Josephus,* trans. and commentary, Steve Mason. Boston:
    Brill Academic Publishers, 2003.
Katz, Steven T. *The Cambridge History of Judaism.* Vol. 4. *The Late Roman-Rabbinic
    Period.* Cambridge: Cambridge University Press, 2006.
Kaufman, Stephen A., "Aramaic." In *The Semitic Languages,* ed. Robert Hetzron,
    pp. 114–30. London: Routledge, 1997.
Kessler, Rainer. *The Social History of Ancient Israel: An Introduction.* Minneapolis,
    MN: Fortress Press, 2008.
La Bianca, Oystein S. "Subsistence Pastoralism." In *Near Eastern Archaeology: A Reader,*
    ed. Suzanne Richard, pp. 116–23. Winona Lake, IN: Eisenbrauns, 2003.
Le Deaut, R. *The Message of the New Testament and the Aramaic Bible (Targum),* trans.
    Stephen F. Miletic. Rome: Biblical Institute Press, 1982.
Levine, Lee I. *Ancient Synagogues Revealed.* Jerusalem: Israel Exploration Society,
    1982.
———. *The Galilee in Late Antiquity.* New York: Jewish Theological Seminary of
    America, 1992.
Lim, Timothy H., and the Centre for Christian Origins. *The Dead Sea Scrolls in Their
    Historical Context.* Edinburgh: T & T Clark, 2000.
MacAdam, Henry Innes. *Studies in the History of the Roman Province of Arabia: The
    Northern Sector.* BAR International Series, 295. Oxford: Biblical Archaeology
    Review, 1986.
Magness, Jodi. *The Archaeology of Qumran and the Dead Sea Scrolls: Studies in the
    Dead Sea Scrolls and Related Literature.* Grand Rapids, MI: William B. Eerd-
    mans, 2002.
Matthews, Victor H. "Everyday Life." In *Near Eastern Archaeology: A Reader,* ed.
    Suzanne Richard, pp. 157–63. Winona Lake, IN: Eisenbrauns, 2003.
Milson, David. *Art and Architecture of the Synagogue in Late Antique Palestine: In the
    Shadow of the Church.* Leiden: Brill, 2007.
Neusner, Jacob. *Judaism in the Beginning of Christianity.* Philadelphia: Fortress Press,
    1984.
———. *The Yerushalmi—The Talmud of the Land of Israel: An Introduction.* Northvale,
    NJ: J. Aronson, 1993.
———, and Bruce Chilton. *In Quest of the Historical Pharisees.* Waco, TX: Baylor
    University Press, 2007.
Painter, K. S. *Churches Built in Ancient Times: Recent Studies in Early Christian Ar-
    chaeology.* Specialist studies of the Mediterranean, vol. 1. London: Society of
    Antiquaries of London, 1994.

Rajak, Tessa. *Josephus, the Historian and His Society*. London: Duckworth, 1983.

Reicke, Bo Ivar. *The New Testament Era: The World of the Bible from 500 B.C. to A.D. 100*. Philadelphia: Fortress Press, 1975.

Rendsburg, Gary A. "Semitic Languages." In *Near Eastern Archaeology: A Reader*, ed. Suzanne Richard, pp. 71–73. Winona Lake, IN: Eisenbrauns, 2003.

Richard, Suzanne, ed. *Near Eastern Archaeology: A Reader*. Winona Lake, IN: Eisenbrauns, 2003.

Saldarini, Anthony J. "Babatha's Story." *Biblical Archaeology Review* 24, 1998: 28–39.

———. *Pharisees, Scribes and Sadducees in Palestinian Society*. Edinburgh: T. & T. Clark, 1989.

Schwartz, Seth. *Imperialism and Jewish Society, 200 B.C.E. to 640 C.E.: Jews, Christians, and Muslims from the Ancient to the Modern World*. Princeton, N.J.: Princeton University Press, 2001.

Scott, J. Julius. *Customs and Controversies: Intertestamental Jewish Backgrounds of the New Testament*. Grand Rapids, MI: Baker Books, 1995.

———. *Jewish Backgrounds of the New Testament*. Grand Rapids, MI: Baker Books, 2000.

Shanks, Hershel. *Understanding the Dead Sea Scrolls: A Reader from the* Biblical Archaeology Review. New York: Random House, 1992.

Smith, George Adam. *The Historical Geography of the Holy Land*. London: Hodder and Stoughton, 24th ed., 1920.

Steiner, Richard C. "Ancient Hebrew." In *The Semitic Languages*, ed. Robert Hetron, pp. 145–73. London: Routledge, 1997.

Stewart, Aubrey, and Charles William Wilson. *Itinerary from Bordeaux to Jerusalem*. London: Committee of the Palestine Exploration Fund, 1887.

Urman, Dan, and Paul Virgil McCracken Flesher. *Ancient Synagogues: Historical Analysis and Archaeological Discovery*. Studia Post-Biblica, vol. 47. Leiden: E. J. Brill, 1995.

VanderKam, James C. *The Dead Sea Scrolls Today*. Grand Rapids, MI: Eerdmans, 1994.

Whiston, William. *The Works of Josephus*. Cheapside: William Milner, 1850.

Wise, Michael Owen, Martin G. Abegg, and Edward M. Cook. *The Dead Sea Scrolls: A New Translation*. San Francisco: Harper San Francisco, 1996.

INTERNET SOURCES

Bible History Online. Rusty Russell, private company, home page http://www.bible-history.com/gives an extensive amount of material online, although without critical review. For an illustration of Herod the Great's Temple, see http://www.bible-history.com/jewishtemple/JEWISH_TEMPLEHerods_Temple_Illustration.htm.

Christian Classics Ethereal Library at Calvin College, Grand Rapids, Michigan, http://www.ccel.org/j/josephus/works/JOSEPHUS.HTM. The site provides the translation of Josephus, a primary nonbiblical source for the first century B.C.E.–C.E. by William Whiston.

Early Christian Writings. Peter Kirby, private company, home page http://www.earlychristianwritings.com/. The site provides a collection material from the first through the third centuries C.E., not just the canonical Christian writings, but Jewish, Early Church Fathers, Apocrypha, and Gnostics.

Gnostic Society of Los Angelus. Dr. Stephan Hoeller, private company, home page http://gnosis.org/library.html, for the library http://www.webcom.com/ ~gnosis/library/scroll.htm. Material with commentary and histories of the Dead Sea Scrolls from the Gnostic Society Library, providing material from the Nag Hammadi Library as well as other sources.

Holyland Model of Ancient Jerusalem. Hans Kroch, owner of Holyland Hotel Jerusalem, completed a model of Ancient Jerusalem in 1967 with the help of professor Avi Yonah of the Hebrew University. See http://www.holyland network.com/temple/model.htm. This online model gives an interactive model of ancient Jerusalem during the time of the Second Temple at the start of the Jewish Rebellion in 66 C.E.

Institute for Jewish Studies at the Hebrew University of Jerusalem, http://orion. mscc.huji.ac.il/. The site gives material about the Dead Sea Scrolls from the Orion center in Jerusalem, part of the Institute for Jewish Studies at the Hebrew University of Jerusalem, and promotes research on all aspects of the Dead Sea Scrolls.

Internet Sacred Text Archive. John Bruno Hare, private company, home page http://www.sacred-texts.com/index.htm. The site gives a 1918 English translation of the Babylonian Talmud, translated by Michael L. Rodkinson, http://www.sacred-texts.com/jud/talmud.htm

Jewish National and University Library and the Hebrew University of Jerusalem, http://jnul.huji.ac.il/dl/maps/jer/. This site provides images and maps of ancient Jerusalem that were compiled by the Jewish National and University Library and the Hebrew University of Jerusalem.

LacusCurtius. Bill Thayer, hosted on the Web site of the University of Chicago, http://penelope.uchicago.edu/Thayer/E/Roman/home.html. This site provides useful material covering Roman history including sources in both the original language and translations.

Library of Congress, Washington D.C., http://www.ibiblio.org/expo/deadsea. scrolls.exhibit/intro.html. Provides an introduction to the Dead Sea Scrolls for an exhibit at the Library of Congress. The site provides images and histories of the community and the scrolls.

VIDEO AND MOVIES

Barabbas (1961). Director, Richard Fleischer; writers, Christopher Fry (screenplay) and Pär Lagerkvist (novel). Release date October 10, 1962 (USA). Dino de Laurentiis Cinematografica.

Ben-Hur (1959). Director, William Wyler; writers, Lew Wallace (novel) and Karl Tunberg. Release date November 18, 1959 (USA). Metro-Goldwyn-Mayer (MGM).

Demetrius and the Gladiators (1954). Director, Delmer Daves; writers, Lloyd C. Douglas (characters in *The Robe*) and Philip Dunne (written by). Release date, June 18, 1954 (USA). Twentieth Century-Fox Film Corporation.

I, Claudius (1976). director, Herbert Wise; writers, Robert Graves (novels) and Jack Pulman. Release date, September 20, 1976 (UK), November 6, 1977 (USA). British Broadcasting Corporation, UK, TV miniseries.

Jesus of Nazareth (1977). Director, Franco Zeffirelli; writing credits, Anthony Burgess, Suso Cecchi d'Amico, Franco Zeffirelli, and David Butler (additional dialogue). Release date April 3, 1977 (USA). Incorporated Television Company (ITC), TV miniseries.

King of Kings (1961). Director, Nicholas Ray; writer, Philip Yordan. Release date October 30, 1961 (USA). Samuel Bronston Productions.

Masada (1981). Director, Boris Sagal; writers, Ernest K. Gann and Joel Oliansky. Release date April 5, 1981 (USA). Arnon Milchan Productions, ABC TV miniseries.

The Passion of the Christ (2004). Director, Mel Gibson; writers, Benedict Fitzgerald (screenplay) and Mel Gibson (screenplay). Release date February 25, 2004 (USA). Icon Productions.

Quo Vadis (1951). Director, Mervyn LeRoy; writers, S. N. Behrman (screenplay) and Sonya Levien (screenplay). Release date, November 8, 1951 (USA). Metro-Goldwyn-Mayer (MGM).

The Robe (1953). Director, Henry Koster; writers (WGA), Philip Dunne (screenplay), Lloyd C. Douglas (novel), and Gina Kaus (adaptation). Release date September 16, 1953 (USA). Twentieth Century-Fox Film Corporation.

INDEX

Agriculture, 24–25, 52, 80–82, 87, 94, 112, 120

Alexander the Great, King of Macedon, 4, 5, 20–21, 23, 26–27, 34, 38–39, 120–21

Alexandria, 4, 5, 35, 39, 80, 97, 113

Ancient Semitic, 32–33

Angels, 63–64, 96

Antioch, 4, 28, 72, 85, 115–16, 130

Antiochus III, King of Syria, 5–6, 117

Antiochus IV, King of Syria, 6, 11, 23, 121

Antipater, 8, 125–26

Antony, Mark, 8–9, 25, 45, 87, 121, 124–25

Arabia, 2–3, 27, 31, 80, 116

Archelaus, 23, 117, 119, 121

Art, 39–41, 49–50, 129

Asia Minor, 2, 4, 8, 14, 19, 28–30, 36–38, 95, 115–16, 123, 128, 130

Astrology, 52–54, 63

Augustus, Emperor, 11, 15, 29, 40, 49, 87, 109, 112; biography, 124–25; relations with Herod, 8–10, 117, 119, 121

Babatha, 95–96

Babylon, 4–6, 22, 24, 120

Babylonia, 4, 9, 21, 23–24, 28, 30, 32, 39, 43, 47, 62, 121

Bar Kochba, 25, 60, 65

Bethlehem, 19, 20, 53, 119

Bible, 5, 31–33, 35, 40, 69, 89–90, 92, 132

Biblical Passages: Acts, 19:23, 83; Deuteronomy, 6:4–9, 131; Deuteronomy, 11:13–21, 131; Deuteronomy, 24:1, 106–7; Exodus, 11–14, 51; Exodus, 12:15–28, 51; Exodus, 13:1–16, 131; Exodus, 19–20, 52; Exodus, 21:10, 106; Exodus, 23:16, 88; Exodus, 25:3–40, 47; Isaiah, 1:8, 101; John, 1:38, 37; John, 2:1–11, 103; John, 3:1–3, 37; John, 4:16–18, 103; John, 5:2–18, 100; John, 8:48, 23; John, 9:7, 100; John, 18:10, 108; John, 18:12, 82; Leviticus, 23:9–14, 88; Leviticus, 23:23–25, 52; Luke, 1:14, 80; Luke, 1:26–36, 64; Luke, 2:4, 19; Luke, 2:13–15, 64; Luke, 2:41–51, 63, 99; Luke, 3:10–14, 86; Luke, 4:16–21, 35; Luke, 4:16–22, 49, 132; Luke, 4:44, 48; Luke, 5:17, 71; Luke, 5:27–32, 78; Luke, 6:15, 65; Luke,

7:30, 71; Luke, 8:5–8, 87, 81; Luke,
    9:51, 23; Luke, 10:23–37, 85; Luke,
    10:30–35, 1; Luke, 11:51, 100; Luke,
    12:36–39, 75; Luke, 19:45–46, 83;
    Luke, 21:5, 76; Luke, 22:52, 82;
    Luke, 22:56, 84; Mark, 1:16–20, 78;
    Mark, 6:45, 22; Mark, 9:5, 37; Mark,
    10:2–9, 107; Mark, 10:11–12, 107;
    Mark, 11:15–19, 79; Mark, 12:1–11,
    80; Mark, 13:1–2, 76; Mark, 13:1–3,
    43; Mark, 14:47, 85; Matthew,
    1:20, 64; Matthew, 2:1–12, 53;
    Matthew, 2:13, 64; Matthew, 2:16,
    10; Matthew, 4:7, 100; Matthew,
    4:10, 100; Matthew, 4:18–20, 20;
    Matthew, 8:5, 29; Matthew, 8:23–27,
    78; Matthew, 12:9, 48; Matthew,
    13:55, 20; Matthew, 16:13–17, 57;
    Matthew, 17:1–8, 101; Matthew,
    19:1–9, 107; Matthew, 20:1–16,
    80, 94; Matthew, 21:13–17, 79;
    Matthew, 21:33–41, 94; Matthew,
    21:42, 100; Matthew, 23:35, 100;
    Matthew, 22:16–21, 58; Matthew,
    22:17–21, 117, 118; Matthew,
    26:25, 37; Matthew, 26:47–50, 101;
    Matthew, 26:51–52, 82; Matthew,
    27:27, 101; Matthew, 27:33, 101;
    Matthew, 27:63, 101; Matthew, 28:6,
    101; Matthew, 31:8, 101; Proverbs,
    15:17, 89
Byblos, 27, 34

Caesarea Maritime, 17, 98, 100,
    113–15, 118; built by Herod the
    Great, 3, 9, 15–16, 76, 80, 123, 126;
    capital, 10, 122
Caiaphas, 11, 32, 54–55, 101
Cana, 21, 80
Capernaum, 21, 48
Celebrations, 51–52
Children, 53, 104–6, 108, 110–11
Christian, 67, 85, 91; beliefs, 72–73,
    108, 110, 112; community, 30, 49,
    100, 116, 128–29; language, 31;
    messiah, 71, 128; separation from
    Judaism, 57–58, 60; structures, 48,
    71, 97, 115; writers, 10, 14

Christianity, 12–14, 35–36, 40, 53,
    70–73, 95, 115, 124, 127–30
Cities, 113–15
Claudius, Emperor, 11, 17, 30, 116
Cleopatra, Queen of Egypt, 9, 39, 87,
    125–26
Constantine, Emperor, 101, 109, 130
Cooking, 81, 83–85, 88, 91
Crassus, M. Licinius, 8, 78
Crops, 88–92
Cyprus, 14, 30, 116, 130
Cyrus, King of Persia, 5, 22

Damascus, 9, 21, 27, 115–16
Damascus Scroll, sect, 68–70
David, King of Israel, 4, 19, 23, 24, 26,
    58–59, 99, 101
Dead Sea, 2, 3, 4, 26, 95
Dead Sea Scrolls, 35, 65, 68, 131, 133
Didache, 71, 73
Diet, 88, 89, 91; dietary rules, 20, 73,
    95, 128–29
Diocletian, Gaius, Emperor, 36, 130
Divorce, 105–8
Dyes, 93

Edom, 5, 26, 32
Egypt, 21, 24, 27, 31, 34, 38–39, 79–80,
    88, 90, 93, 97, 99, 110, 120; Jesus in,
    64; Jews in, 4–5, 51–53, 107; position
    with Syria, 2, 5–7, 9, 19, 25; Romans
    in, 8, 17, 30, 82, 125, 126, 130
Eleazar, rebel leader, 12, 13, 16, 134–35
Elephantine, 107
Ephesus, 4, 28, 113, 115–16, 130
Essenes, 63, 65–66, 69–70; baptism, 72;
    not mentioned in New Testament,
    71, 128, 131

Family, 103–6, 108–13
Farming, 81
Fishing, 19, 78
Flocks, 83, 92
Fortress Antonia, 9, 11, 13, 16, 25, 45,
    114, 126

Galilee, 16, 19–22, 36, 78, 91–92, 97;
    conversion of Jews, 10; geography,

2, 4, 7; Herod's rule, 8, 125–26; nationalism, 60, 65, 71, 127

Geography. *See* New Testament

Grain, 3, 19, 50, 82, 84, 88–89, 91, 120, 123, 125

Grapes, 80–81, 90–91, 94

Greece, 2, 4, 14, 21, 28–29, 38, 95, 99, 116–17, 120, 128, 130

Hadrian, 25, 100

Hasmonaeans, 6, 8, 32–33

Hellenism, 5, 27, 38–40, 60–61, 63, 123–24, 127–28

Herod Agrippa I, 11–12, 17, 115

Herod Antipas, 10–12, 21–22, 25, 49, 127

Herod the Great, 20, 26–27, 34, 39, 49, 106, 110, 125–27; constructs Caesarea, 3, 9, 15–16, 114, 118, 123; Fortress Antonia, 25, 45–46; Jesus, 53, 58; Masada, 13, 123; rule of, 8–10, 20, 23, 60, 62, 119–21; successors, 10–11, 22–23, 117, 121, 124; Temple, 9, 43–44, 46, 51, 76, 115, 133

Herodians, 110

Herodias, 21

Hillel, 9, 106–8

Idumaea, 5, 7–8, 13, 25

Italy, 2, 4, 29, 54, 84, 99, 116, 123–25, 128, 130

James, 20, 73, 128

Jericho, 1, 3, 9, 10

Jerusalem, 1, 3, 7–8, 23, 34, 63, 66–67, 81; Herod, 9, 118, 120–21, 126; History, 6, 25, 113–16; Pilate, 11, 122; position in religion, 22–24, 32–33, 36–37, 48, 70, 73, 98–99, 107; siege and destruction, 12–17, 27, 90, 58–60, 69, 71, 100–101, 128; Temple, 4, 8, 24–25, 43–45, 47, 62–63, 76, 133

Jesus: death, 25, 45, 52, 71; family, 20, 53, 63, 75–76, 119; followers, 20, 23–24, 65, 78–79, 84, 108, 115, 128; language, 32–33, 35, 37, 132; message, 29, 63–64, 83, 106–8,

118, 128; messiah, 57–60, 71, 73, 130; parable, 1, 20, 43, 57, 88, 103; synagogue, 48–49; travel, 2, 21–22, 27, 63, 99, 127

Jewish history, 4–10, 19

Jewish marriage, 51, 103–6

Jewish Rebellion, 13–14, 16–18, 27, 59–60, 66, 112, 128, 130

John, Saint, 20, 101

John Gischala, 16

John Hyrcanus I, 7, 20

John Hyrcanus II, 7–9, 65

John the Baptist, 21–22, 67, 86, 127

Jordan River, 2–4, 9, 113

Joseph, husband of Mary, 19–20, 53, 64, 75, 105, 119

Josephus, 16–18; account of Jerusalem, 13–14, 43, 122; Caesarea, 18, 98; Jewish groups, 62–63, 65, 70, 133; rebellion, 19, 27, 49, 133–35; synagogues, 48

Judea, 19–28, 63, 71, 119, 128; geography, 1–2, 4, 26; History, 4–5, 7–8, 10–12, 58–59; language, 32–33, 36; rule, 9–10, 13, 65

Julius Caesar, 8, 78, 112, 116, 124–25

Kohen, 50–51

Korban, 50

Language, 23, 31–38, 40; Aramaic, 23, 32–37, 40, 96, 115, 132; Greek, 5, 31–37, 40, 48, 95–96, 115, 132; Hebrew, 5, 23, 31–37, 68–69, 132; Latin, 31, 33–34, 36–37

Leather, 69, 76–77, 93–94

Luke, Saint, 55, 99

Maccabees, 8, 58, 64, 69, 127

Macedonian, 5, 21, 38–39, 116, 125

Magdalene, Mary, 70

Magic, 52–54, 63

Mark, 43, 107

Markets, 79, 82, 96–97, 99, 114

Marriage, 103–11

Mary, Mother of Jesus, 53, 64, 105, 119

Masada, 9, 13, 27, 59, 123, 133–35

Matthew, Saint, 53

Mediterranean, 2, 5, 14, 27, 40, 63; history, 7–8, 12, 15, 28; trade, 3, 9, 20, 22, 37–38, 77, 80, 97, 123

Menorah, 7, 13, 17, 46–48

Merchants, 97, 110, 113–14; Gospels, 2, 20, 80; language, 33, 36, 40; occupations, 76–79, 82; trade, 20, 25, 37, 80, 123

Messiah, 10–11, 16, 57–61, 65, 71, 73, 96, 127–28, 130

Mishnah, 33, 83, 85

Moses, 11, 22–23, 47, 50, 52, 61–62, 64, 96, 99, 101

Nazareth, 19–21, 35

Nebuchadnezzar, 4, 22

Nero, 13, 17, 40, 116, 119

New Testament, 14, 20, 31, 35; divorce, 106, 108; family, 103, 108–10, 112; geography, 1, 2, 4, 28, 37, 40, 81–82; groups, 20, 23, 30, 39–40, 64, 70–71; messiah, 57–58, 63; occupations, 75, 103; rebellion, 13; religion, 35, 39, 52–53, 129; Temple, 43, 49

Occupations: blacksmith, 83, 113; builder, 75–76; carpenter, 75–76, 84, 113; clothing worker, 76–77; cook, 84–85; coppersmith, 83; day worker, 94; goat herder, 83; goldsmith, 83; leather worker, 76–77; potter, 20, 69, 83–85, 131; sail maker, 84; shepherd, 80, 83, 92, 99; shopkeeper, 84; silk worker, 77; silversmith, 83; smiths, 83, 85, 113; stonemason, 76, 113; tax collector, 78–80; viticulture, 80

Octavian. *See* Augustus, Emperor

Olives, 3, 47, 81, 90–91, 94

Ostia, 49, 80

Palestine, 2–4, 5, 19–21, 28, 36, 87–88, 99; Diaspora, 40, 62, 71; history, 9–15; synagogues, 48

Parthia, 6, 8, 11, 17, 21, 28, 31, 36, 122

Paul, 86, 115–16; Christian communities, 30; language, 31, 35, 40; profession, 162, 76, 85, 194;

synagogues, 49; travels, 14–15, 28–29, 84, 115; views, 24, 108, 122

Peraea, 2, 9–10, 13

Peter, Saint, 20, 28, 49, 52, 57, 72, 84, 101, 108

Pharisees, 1, 7, 9–10, 20, 50, 61–65; divorce, 107; views, 70–71, 127–29

Philip, son of Herod, 10–11, 21–22

Philo, 46, 62, 122

Phoenicia, 23–24, 27–28, 32, 34, 39, 93

Pilate, 11, 54–55, 122; Jesus, 25, 58, 101; language, 33–34

Pilgrimage, 9, 24, 36–37, 99–101

Pompey, 8–9, 23, 121, 123

Prostitution, 79

Ptolemies, 4–7, 38–39, 120–21

Qumran, 65–69, 131–32

Rabbis, 36–37, 63, 83, 85, 98, 106, 111

Red Sea, 2, 3, 51

Resurrection, 21, 61–62, 64, 70–71, 73, 127

Romanization, 123–24

Roman occupation, 117–19

Rome, 6, 59, 86; control, 7, 9–10, 15, 23, 25, 45–46, 122–23; culture, 21, 49

Sabbath, 6, 35, 50, 64, 72–73, 88, 94–95, 100, 129

Sacrifice, 6, 10, 12, 23–25, 39, 44, 50–52, 82, 85, 92

Sadducees, 1, 61–62; political, 7–10, 50, 128; temple, 25, 70–71, 130; views, 62–65, 70, 127

Samaria, 2, 4, 22–25, 28, 61, 85; history, 7–11, 13; language, 33–34

Samaritan, 1, 2, 5, 23–24

Sanhedrin, 7, 9–10, 20, 55, 66, 114, 125

Scribes, 7, 70–71

Seasons, 51, 87–88, 91–92, 129

Sejanus, 10–11

Seleucids, 5, 7, 38, 59, 64, 114–15, 117, 120–21, 127; Rome, 8, 10–12, 23, 28, 49, 77

Sidon, 23, 27–28, 34

Simon Peter. *See* Peter

Simon Zealot, 59

Slaves, 14, 59–60, 67, 82, 85, 94, 108–13

Soldiers, 1, 15, 38, 64, 86, 100, 109, 116, 122, 124
Solomon, King of Israel, 4, 20, 24, 43, 46–47, 58, 99, 100
Synagogues, 5, 11, 15, 33–37, 39, 43, 47–50, 62–63, 70–71, 73, 76, 101, 113–14, 128, 132
Syria, 2, 24, 30, 32, 80, 95; relations with Egypt, 5, 19, 25, 27–28

Tabernacle, 46–47, 52, 90
Talmud, 43, 48, 82, 96, 98–99
Targum, 33–35
Tarsus, 4, 29, 62, 76, 115
Taverns, 84
Taxes, 119–21
Temple, 9, 25, 43–45, 76, 85, 107; authority, 98; Essenes, 70; Jerusalem, 4, 25, 115, 122; religion, 6–7, 10, 11–12, 46–47, 73; sacrifice, 50–52; Sadducees, 61–63, 131;

siege, 12, 16, 24, 47, 115, 132; travel, 99
Temple economy, 25, 82–83
Tiberias, 10, 21
Tiberius, 10–11, 54, 122, 125
Titus, 12–13, 16–18, 46–47
Town government, 97–98
Towns, 97–98, 113–15
Transjordanian, 21–22, 92
Tyre, 3, 27–28, 34, 77, 93

Vespasian, 13, 17, 27, 47, 59
Villages, 15, 82, 96, 113
Vines, 3, 20, 80–81, 90–91, 94, 101

Yarn, 77, 80, 93

Zealot, 1, 64–65, 71; follower of Jesus, 59; nationalism, 10, 16, 51, 121, 128

About the Author

JAMES W. ERMATINGER is dean of the College of Liberal Arts at Bloomsburg University, Bloomsburg, Pennsylvania. He is author of *Daily Life of
Christians in Ancient Rome* (Greenwood, 2007), *The Decline and Fall of the
Roman Empire* (2004), and *Economic Reforms of Diocletian* (1996), as well as
other articles on late Roman history.